PRAISE FOR *THE WHITE COAT ENTREPRENEUR*

"Building on his own life experience, Dr. Edwin Williams has crafted an excellent and important book that should be required reading for every physician aspiring to start or already running a private practice."

—William H. Truswell, MD, FACS, past president of AAFPRS

"Dr. Williams shares very valuable points throughout this book, from the hard truths about budgeting to the passion required to build a successful business, including training successors for management so the owner is rewarded by being able to spend less time and eventually exit profitability."

—David J. Prescott, founder of Integra Optics, serial entrepreneur

"Ed has been the most singularly exceptional mentor for me in all aspects of my life, including business (for which he awakened a deep passion in me), surgery, patient care, leadership, and integrity, and I was fortunate to learn from observing him as his fellow for a year. Please read this important book that is filled with masterful pearls and life lessons, because when Ed speaks I listen attentively to his every word."

—Samuel M. Lam, MD, FACS

T0098693

THE
WHITE
COAT
ENTREPRENEUR

THE
WHITE
COAT
ENTREPRENEUR

**Master Business So You Can Work Less, Earn More, and
Exit Successfully While Maintaining a Balanced Life**

EDWIN WILLIAMS, MD

Advantage.

Published by Advantage, Charleston, South Carolina.
Member of Advantage Media Group.

ADVANTAGE is a registered trademark, and the Advantage colophon is a trademark of Advantage Media Group, Inc.

Printed in the United States of America.

10 9 8 7 6 5 4 3 2 1

ISBN: 978-1-64225-106-7
LCCN: 2019916748

Cover design by Jamie Earley.
Layout design by George Stevens.

This publication is designed to provide accurate and authoritative information in regard to the subject matter covered. It is sold with the understanding that the publisher is not engaged in rendering legal, accounting, or other professional services. If legal advice or other expert assistance is required, the services of a competent professional person should be sought.

Advantage Media Group is proud to be a part of the Tree Neutral® program. Tree Neutral offsets the number of trees consumed in the production and printing of this book by taking proactive steps such as planting trees in direct proportion to the number of trees used to print books. To learn more about Tree Neutral, please visit **www.treeneutral.com**.

Advantage Media Group is a publisher of business, self-improvement, and professional development books and online learning. We help entrepreneurs, business leaders, and professionals share their Stories, Passion, and Knowledge to help others Learn & Grow. Do you have a manuscript or book idea that you would like us to consider for publishing? Please visit **advantagefamily.com** or call **1.866.775.1696**.

To my father, Ed Williams Jr., who taught by me by example the importance of an extremely strong work ethic and never settling or being complacent in business. At times I would question my intelligence, because I was not a strong high school student. However, because of this work ethic I was taught, I always knew that I could work harder than the competition and come out on top. He taught me the importance of living well within my means and the desire to think big and take risks while others would be comfortable to sit on the sidelines. To you, Dad, I dedicate this book.

CONTENTS

INTRODUCTION

Growing up, I'd always had entrepreneur blood in me. My grandfather was a successful business tycoon in Manhattan. My parents had their hands in businesses, too, and always inspired me. With all the business-minded people around me, my own entrepreneurial spirit rose early. By age fourteen, I was raising a dozen beef cattle on my own, and by high school I'd saved up enough to buy ten run-down cars that I fixed and sold at a profit.

You'll learn how I got into medicine later in this book, but even when I chose that career path and graduated med school, what tugged at my curiosity most was the business aspect of running a physician practice. With this curiosity came another realization: there was an entire world of knowledge to be mastered beyond anything I'd ever learned in med school if I wanted to see my dreams of running a successful physician practice take root.

With this insightful thought tucked in my mind, I began my career by observing educated, sophisticated business friends sell companies and walk away wealthy by age forty. I remember thinking to myself, "Heck, these folks are no smarter than I am, and I'd rather do what they're doing instead of just working for someone else." To do that, I knew I needed to understand business better than I did. Systematically I began to educate myself and build my practice based on what I was learning from other smart, successful people.

The end result? A twenty-one-thousand-square-foot facility with multiple surgeons and several physicians and ownership of a practice that's in the top 1 percent of the country based on our revenue and profitability. Today, at age sixty, there's no need for me to work. I'm no longer chasing the next face-lift to see a bump in my revenue.

All the knowledge I've gained and the discipline I've practiced over the years has given me the freedom to do what I want with my time.

So now that I do have that time, why did I choose to use it writing this book?

Part of it is the business lover inside me wanting to discuss my passion. Anyone who knows me knows I love the entrepreneurial aspect of what we do as physicians. But the other part of it is to deliver guidance and hope to other aspiring physician entrepreneurs who are discouraged by their peers. Every year I see an outpouring of students and aspiring physicians grow dispirited at the notion of launching their own practice or any business for that matter. They work entirely too hard physically, suffer burnout, make blunders, and see their businesses crash and burn.

→ There's a common misconception floating out there that you can't be a good doctor and a good businessperson.

Some of them don't even get to the point of owning their own practice; they end up throwing in the proverbial towel and calling it quits before they've even gotten their hands wet as physicians. This book is to address all that and more.

For instance, there's a common misconception floating out there that you can't be a good doctor and a good businessperson. I disagree. And in this book, I'll prove that it's more than possible to be both. I'm writing this to inspire those who need inspiration, guide those who need guidance, and mentor those who need to be mentored. All you have to do is understand business and know how to adopt a work–life balance—both of which are topics, among others, that I'll touch on in this book. I want to write this to encourage younger physicians to preserve this noble profession we've signed up for. My hope is to enable you to follow in my footsteps while helping you avoid my mistakes. I want you to make all the right choices without suffering any of the most common failures. Sure, medicine as a profession in America is changing; however, where there is change there is opportunity. So flip the page, and let the journey begin.

CHAPTER 1

MY STORY

I don't remember the eighties. Not the music, the sitcoms, or the politics. When I look back at that era, it feels as though I was living in a parallel universe, hard at work trying to make the grade for med school. It was a challenge I enjoyed and one that required every ounce of my efforts, which I didn't mind.

Meanwhile, ask any of my nonmedical professional friends, and they'll recall that decade very differently—because they were the ones out attending concerts, partying to Michael Jackson, hanging out, and dating.

Once my thirteen years of college medical school, residency, and fellowship were up, I emerged, feeling like I'd entered a different world. I had learned so much, more than I'd ever learned in my entire life combined, and in the process I'd given up the opportunity to make friends or have any semblance of a social life. At the time I understood this to be a sacrifice worth making because I knew the opportunities forsaken were just short-term losses that would, ultimately, bring me the long-term gain of inching that much closer toward my dreams of becoming a doctor.

If you'd asked me several years prior to then whether I could have imagined or truly understood the intensity of pursuing my MD (doctor of medicine), I would have probably paused. In reality, at the time, I had no clue what doctors had to go through to make it to the finish line because, truth be told, physicians behold a profession more unique than any other in this world.

WHY PHYSICIANS ARE DIFFERENT

Teachers, real estate agents, dentists, chefs—no other profession out there is quite like a physician's.

Imagine pouring years, money, and effort into your profession. Imagine investing as much time—or more—in studying as you would in a full-time job. Imagine willingly relinquishing simple luxuries such as hanging out with friends or enjoying a movie on the couch on an ordinary Saturday night. Imagine waiting decades to see the fruits of your labor. Collectively, these statements describe what physicians sign up for. This is the type of life they become intimately familiar with—one they willingly embrace so they can claim access to a respected profession.

Becoming a physician means signing on the dotted line to forgo a few pleasures early on in exchange for a brighter, more promising future much later in life, maybe in your forties.

The sacrifices test your commitment to the profession early on. From the onset, aspiring physicians not only have limited social lives but they also often miss out on important life milestones such as family gatherings, birthdays, and holidays as they commit themselves wholeheartedly to studying so they can earn the grades. Because if they're not at the top of their classes, they won't have a shadow of a chance of getting into medical school. Once they're in, however, the sacrifices don't end. Medical graduates typically enter into a three-to-five-year residency, and in several cases residents don't cap out at a certain number of hours, meaning they invest an exorbitant number of hours at work. Once residency is over, doctors have the opportunity to further distinguish themselves by pursuing fellowships, some of which last one to two years at up to eighty hours a week. Although this isn't true of every residency and fellowship, it holds true for most competitive surgical ones.

By this point, most of these aspiring physicians are in their early thirties and witness friends who aren't in the medical field enjoying life, starting families, and perhaps even rolling around town in fancy cars. These peers have already invested several years in their careers and are gaining positive momentum, seeing upward mobility at work. To top it off, most of them are financially stable—in most cases more so than the physician.

→ Many people, medical students included, presume that because physicians make a killing, they're predestined to be wealthy.

Does it get worse? Unfortunately, yes.

Many people, medical students included, presume that because physicians make a killing, they're predestined to be wealthy. To some extent, aspiring physicians start feeling entitled to this money early on after all the hard work they pour into their education and work. They start spending and driving up debt, confident things will turn around for them soon enough once the money starts to flow. The cherry on top: The majority of them already hold large sums of student debt to the tune of hundreds of thousands of dollars.

Unfortunately, by the time the money finally does start rolling in, the debt has amassed to crazy amounts, leaving the physician to slowly chip away at it with any leftover portions of their paycheck. Meanwhile, their friends are enjoying luxury homes and international travel with their excess funds.

It sounds like a nightmare—and for many it is. The sacrifices literally don't end, and the most significant one is the sacrifice of time.

Fortunately for me, my story was a little different. I don't think I recalled just how different, however, until my daughter, who is a physician herself, approached me one day and said something that made me realize it.

I still remember her slumping in, looking weary, exhausted, and dispirited. "You know, Dad," she told me, "I've come to the conclusion that if you really want to do well in medical school, you have to let go of life."

Her sentiments elicited a tug of familiarity; in that moment I remembered thinking exactly the same thing when I was a young student.

Although I didn't want to dishearten her by sharing my own similar thoughts, I also wanted to offer honest advice and make sure she was guiding herself toward her true passion, so I chose my words carefully.

"Listen," I told her, "becoming a doctor is like committing to become a professional athlete. It has to be something you absolutely want to do—no one can push or encourage or force you to do it. If you truly want to be successful, that desire has to come all on its own from within you. And yes, there are sacrifices to be made sometimes."

She nodded her agreement but paused contemplatively.

"How come it wasn't like that with you, though, Dad?" she asked. "You went to medical school. Even today you're always studying in your den, but you never missed any of my basketball games. You didn't sacrifice *us*."

I was surprised she'd noticed because kids usually don't think that deep into things. But she was right; I'd never sacrificed them because I'd made a concentrated effort not to, no matter how tough it sometimes was. I was focused on putting my family first from the start because they'd always been my priority.

But what she said next is what really sat with me. "And another thing," she continued, "I'm so glad you taught me what you did about being responsible with money."

My lips tugged up into a soft smile. "Well," I said, "we both really have your grandfather to thank for that. He's a scrapper and always taught me to live conservatively and hustle like I was broke."

And for that I was eternally thankful. My father's financial lessons and fiscal influence over me are what ultimately led to my success as a physician entrepreneur. Looking back at the days I'd stood observing him and taking in his practices, I can honestly say the greatest lessons I learned that contributed to my success weren't the ones I learned from coursework or med school. They're the ones I learned from him.

GROWING UP ON OPEN EARTH

My parents weren't rich or employed by large corporations. They raised me and my siblings in Orange County, New York, a place two hours north of New York City. In this part of the state, there were no skyscrapers or crowds of businessmen pacing the streets in suits and ties. We lived in the quiet suburbs where green hills rolled freely.

My parents were entrepreneurs who dabbled in real estate, vending machines, laundromats—you name it—all in an attempt to put dinner on the table and make a better life than their parents had for them. My father grew up too fast trying to provide for his siblings and family, picking up odd jobs and, ultimately, starting several small businesses in the process. You could, I guess, say he had an entrepreneurial spirit at a very young age—like me.

Growing up, I knew my parents didn't have a lot of money, and my father certainly wasn't the type to hand me over any. So at the age of fourteen, I took a job on my neighbor's dairy farm, which I stuck with for the next decade while I attended college and then medical school. I juggled about twenty-five to thirty hours a week on the farm during the school year and in the summer between seventy and eighty hours. There was no such thing as vacationing for spring break when there were fields to be plowed, rocks to be picked, and way too much work on the farm to be done. Besides how could I possibly even think of vacationing when my dad was working around the clock with all of his small business efforts? Between being a competitive high school wrestler and a helping hand on the farm, I learned how to work hard and efficiently.

Never grow complacent— hustle like you're broke.
Dr. Edwin Williams

As far as school goes, that was a different story altogether. Contrary to what most people may believe, I was never a star student. Far from it. In fact, my parents themselves weren't academics by any means.

Both had studied until high school, which on my dad's side of the family was a huge accomplishment worthy of celebration; he was the only one out of seven siblings to graduate.

Once he married my mom, he started working for someone else but soon realized that for all the effort he was putting in, the owner was the one making all the money. Seeing potential in business, he quit his job and kicked off on his own as a businessman (more on that in the next chapter).

Essentially, this made us scrappers—we were always scraping by, wondering what tomorrow would bring and how/if we'd get by on the day's earnings.

My parents, like most, desired for me and my siblings to have what they themselves didn't: a strong educational backing resulting in an illustrious career. Early on, they instilled in me the importance of gaining an education to learn everything I possibly could.

I tried my hardest to make them proud. I hung through elementary and middle school by a thread, but high school nearly knocked me off my feet. I didn't have great SAT scores nor did I have the guidance or grades to attend college.

I still recall my high school guidance counselor sitting me down in the latter part of those years and saying, "Listen, Edwin. You don't have what it takes, gradewise at least, to get into a four-year college. My advice to you would be to attend a two-year school, major in science, then try applying to a four-year institution."

That's when I resigned myself to the fact that I wasn't going to become anyone unless I worked deliberately hard. Sure, I didn't have the grades, but thanks to my years on the farm, I was the hardest worker I knew.

Work the hardest became a mantra in my mind, affording me newfound confidence in myself. It's what motivated me to keep my head down and continue hustling until I succeeded.

After graduating high school, I followed the advice of my counselor, matriculating into a two-year college and majoring in chemistry. I was determined to make something of myself, so I worked tirelessly—in the end, I was astonished to find my efforts had paid off. I graduated with a whopping 3.9 grade point average, which got me into Cornell University, much to my utter and complete disbelief.

→ *Work the hardest became a mantra in my mind, affording me newfound confidence in myself.*

Being a Cornell transfer student who was trying to get into medical school proved challenging. To some degree, I feel those years were more difficult than medical school itself because I wasn't a strong student by nature, so I had to work extra hard to learn how to study effectively.

Then came the next minor hurdle: choosing a career path.

Growing up around animals on the farm, I was initially inclined toward becoming a veterinarian. However, it wasn't until after I worked at a small animal hospital that I realized my fondness for big farm animals far surpassed my feelings for the furry little ones. Alongside this struck another realization: there was no way I could expect to make a great living tending to dairy cattle. This conundrum became a known obstacle in my life.

A woman in one of my classes, who is now a practicing internist in Florida, was the one who helped me through this hurdle. "Have you ever considered med school?" she asked one day when I was particularly frustrated about which direction to take.

I pondered her suggestion but wasn't completely sold that medical school was the right decision for me. In either case I thought it was at least worth a shot since I didn't have any other brighter ideas. Fortunately, my grade point average was solid enough for it, and before I knew it, I was in.

MED SCHOOL: FROM DREAM TO REALITY

Once immersed in the world of anatomy, I was surprised to find that I simply couldn't get enough of it. I was drawn in, fascinated with the study of the head and neck. To start, I applied to ENT (ears, nose, and throat) head and neck surgery residency, but somewhere along the way, I stumbled into facial plastic surgery. That's when I really fell in love.

I remember being thrilled about attending the University of Illinois in Chicago for my facial plastic surgery fellowship. Soon, however, I felt miserably homesick. Fortunately, by then I'd learned something new about myself that would help me venture closer to home through a newfound inspiration: I realized I didn't just enjoy *learning* about medical sciences, I also loved *teaching* it.

With this passion burning bright, I trekked homeward toward Albany, New York, where I opened my first-ever solo practice. Tucked just around the bend was also a teaching residency so I could run my practice by day and instruct others about my passion by night.

Although I didn't know a soul nearby, I felt reassured that I had the best of both worlds—a small-city, big-town place that had all the attributes I was looking for; I was somewhat close to Vermont, where I could practice my love for skiing, but was also minutes away from the country, where horses skittered boundless.

While I was busy appreciating the big picture, what I failed to realize was that in setting up my own practice, I wouldn't be welcomed with open arms by the community. Being the new guy in town was not looked upon favorably, and the competition tried viciously to block me in the emergency rooms. I tried to live my early mantra of keeping my head down and working hard. Apart from that, I also tried to be available and to provide the best possible care I could to each and every patient. Soon enough, one patient led to two, two led to three, and so it continued. It took a couple of years, but finally, I gained momentum.

Meanwhile, I continued to pour my energy into teaching, which gave me much satisfaction.

Even several years later, after scrapping my way through emergency rooms and growing my private practice, my passion for mentoring remained—in part due to my firm belief in servitude.

Today, my practice has flourished more than I'd ever anticipated. I've added a group of amazing specialists in the area of plastic surgery. We have a surgery center, a number of separate profit centers, and about seventy-five employees.

Although I've sacrificed many things while studying long hours and relinquishing any form of a personal life, the efforts have paid off. However, the secret behind my real success, as I mentioned to my daughter that day, didn't come from anything I'd learned in school. The reason I'd made sure to give myself so fully to my children wasn't because of coursework. It was all thanks to things I'd gleaned from my parents and from working on the farm. Two of the greatest skills I carry with me today I learned from my father: being fiscally responsible and working harder than anyone else. He is one of the greatest influencers in my life—and a man worthy of his own chapter.

CHAPTER 2

RESETTING THE MIND-SET

How to Think Like a Small Businessperson

O ne day when I was still in grade school, I recall entering the kitchen to catch sight of my dad holding a pitcher of milk in one hand and dumping a heap full of powdered milk into it with the other. This was his way of making it last a little longer.

Like many boys do, I admired my father and aspired to be just like him. I observed his habits and idiosyncrasies to infinitesimal detail, hence the recollection of the milk story. I knew how he dressed, walked, and talked and even how he conducted business.

One thing I could attest to is that as a businessman, my father never sat idle. He made it a point to have his hands in as many ventures as possible, hoping that one day something would take off. He had his money in laundromats, hardware stores, furniture stores, rental apartments—the list went on and on. Essentially, my father was certain to put his dollars behind anything cutting edge at the time.

Despite his efforts, however, our family didn't have much during those early years. We'd always worry, wondering whether the next recession was just around the bend, ready to put our meager savings and livelihood at risk.

My father made sure he stretched every penny to the max through his many inventive tactics. That was our life, and it was one we were content with and used to.

It wasn't until med school that I realized how much of an oddball our socioeconomic status made me against the majority of my classmates and colleagues. Many of them came from parents who held fast to white-collar jobs, made a decent living, and vacationed throughout the year—all boxes my family couldn't checkmark. I couldn't remember my parents ever taking us for a vacation, except the occasional trip to Maryland to visit family. My dad never gave us handouts and not once had I ever splurged a cent on luxuries—only necessities such as food.

In spite of these superficial differences, my colleagues and I mixed well in med school, and I admit I learned a lot. However, the one clear advantage I had over them was that while they knew how to extract their wallets and buy most luxuries without a second thought, I'd mastered budgeting and squeezing every penny out of each dollar down to an art—all thanks to my dad.

Through his skills as a businessman, my father taught me fiscal responsibility. Because tomorrow was always an uncertainty in his chosen profession, frugality is something he practiced with regularity and a skill that soon became second nature to me as well.

These sacrifices would teach me more about being fiscally successful as a physician than anything else. Little did I know that this skill, not my talent as a medical professional, would be the primary reason I'd be approached by private equity time and time again. Little did I know that this skill—not anything I'd gleaned from med school—would be the reason I'd be able to finance a 21,000-square-foot building with a surgery center at the age of thirty-eight, just five years into my practice.

Unfortunately, many people in the medical field don't realize that simply being a successful, intelligent medical professional isn't enough to build a respectable, durable practice. Running a practice requires a key skill set that most medical professionals don't acquire in med school: the skill set of thinking like a business owner. This chapter will unveil business best practices I sourced from my own father so you, too, can adopt them.

However, before we focus on that, you'll need to reset your mind-set to think less like a physician and more like a businessperson. For that, you'll need to banish from your mind four common lies that hold most physicians under their detrimental spell.

THE FOUR BIG MYTHS

Doctors are considered some of the brightest, most respected professionals of any industry, yet many of them struggle as entrepreneurs. I attribute their shortcomings to four big myths. Some of these myths they tell themselves; others are told to them. Regardless of the source, these myths hinder the progress and success of physician entrepreneurs, which means if you're aspiring to be one, you should be aware of them and prepare to release them from your minds before they become the very setbacks that prevent you from achieving your dreams.

Myth #1: Education Is Your Biggest Asset

A brilliant friend of mine once worked as an engineer at General Electric for several years. One day, he came to me in complete awe. "Ed, you won't believe what these people do," he told me. "When GE hires you, they bring you to the area and show you the biggest house you can afford to buy. Because once you're financially committed to that big home and lifestyle, it becomes much more difficult to consider a risky move or opportunity. You're basically stuck in that home—and with GE."

Unfortunately, the same is true when you enter the medical profession. People—neighbors, family members, friends—all dangle a golden apple in front of your eyes. They feed you a lie they don't even know is a lie, telling you that since you're in the medical field, you're set for life. They tell you all you need to do to see the dough roll in is to work. You're told that you're a respected professional and won't ever have to fret about money.

Although these statements may very well be embedded in encouragement and good intent, they're in part responsible for why many doctors fail as entrepreneurs. When ingested repeatedly from multiple sources, these myths begin to take on the form of truth in our minds. In turn, we start to buy into them, squandering other potential opportunities to further learn and improve our skills, because we're so confident that we've acquired the highest education attainable, that we are set for life, and that we have absolutely no need to pursue other knowledge. In turn, we throw potential assets—such as learning how to operate a business when we know we desire to run our own practices one day—to the wayside and treat them secondarily.

However, these myths do more than stifle the entrepreneurial spirit; they also cause us to settle into a lavish lifestyle we're told we deserve and are expected to effortlessly afford.

In rising to these standards, many physicians add on mounds of debt. Attending med school already sets them back hundreds of thousands of dollars in student debt—another ten or fifteen grand more, they figure, won't break the bank. As a result, they splurge on big homes, nice cars, and expensive materialisms. If they have spouses, they're forced to keep up appearances through them as well, so they sidestep the minivans and opt for the Mercedes-Benzes. They feel confident that their high-end professions will rake in the dollars faster than they can spend them, eventually. In hopes of that, they continue adding to their bills and start living outside their means.

This is problematic not only from a personal standpoint but also a professional one. By adding to mountains of preexisting debt, physicians not only decrease their chances of ever seeing their paychecks catch up with their exorbitant lifestyles but also limit their ability to take on future risks as business owners because any form of business, whether a retail shop or a practice, requires the ability to adopt a certain level of risk. Without risk, the chances of seeing rewards are slim to none.

Myth #2: Businesses Are Launched by People with Entrepreneurial Skills

I am a big believer in reading and self-edification. One particular book called *The E-Myth Revisited*, by Michael Gerber, is an excellent one I highly recommend on the topic of business. At its core, the book focuses on debunking the common myth that most businesses are launched by people who possess entrepreneurial skills when, in fact, nothing could be further from the truth. Most businesses are kicked off by people who are simply excellent at their craft—they're what I call strong "technicians." That's problematic, however, because being excellent at a skill, passion, or craft isn't nearly enough to help you run a successful business. A top-notch doctor can't expect to be an exceptional businessperson simply because they're an expert at medicine. To run a business, you must be an expert *at* business, which requires a unique skill set of its own.

> → A top-notch doctor can't expect to be an exceptional businessperson simply because they're an expert at medicine.

Physicians are at a particular loss because they fail to understand this logic. Because they're notoriously reputed to be the smartest of the smart and full of brains and intelligence, most doctors believe that if they have the grit to pass medical school, everything else, including running a practice, should be child's play. With this confidence they launch a practice, expecting that running it will be a breeze. What they usually don't realize until it's too late is that operating a business requires a different kind of smarts that's not necessarily innate or a by-product of intelligence. Instead, it's a product of sufficient *business* knowledge.

Unfortunately, about 90 percent of all businesses fail for this very reason—lack of knowledge (and also lack of capital). This means that if you launch a practice without knowing how to run it, you've already placed yourself at a dangerous disadvantage. (Fortunately, there are ways out of this, which we'll address later in this chapter when we discuss how to avoid being vacuumed into the four big lies.)

Myth #3: Professionals Don't Fail

I remember approaching my father one day when I was nervous about making a particularly large investment. "Dad," I told him, "honestly, I'm a little nervous about spending one hundred thousand dollars on this new laser."

He gave me a cursory glance, completely unfazed, and said, "Ed, it'll be fine. You'll make it work." It was a flippant response but not because he didn't care. In fact, the moment he said those words, I knew exactly what was going through his mind—the same thing that goes through everyone's minds and another common myth society buys into: professionals don't fail.

Being a doctor carries an inherent connotation of guaranteed success.

However, that's perhaps the largest myth. Doctors and professionals can fail; they fail all the time.

→ Doctors and professionals can fail; they fail all the time.

Like most doctors, a physician friend of mine—a brilliant man—fell prey to this mind-set early on in his career. Once he graduated medical school, he partnered with another plastic surgeon for six or seven years. Together, the two of them invested in a state-of-the-art facility in the heart of New York—Manhattan. Although they were renting the space, they were eager in their pursuit and went overboard in excitement, splurging on a plethora of upgrades from costly renovations to unnecessary improvements to pricey lasers. At the end of the day, their total expenditures topped $800,000—and my friend signed the bank loan with his partner, agreeing to be an equal party to that debt.

Unfortunately, shortly afterward, the 2008 financial recession hit. They tanked; they'd ended up overleveraging themselves. In a matter of months, my friend was forced to file bankruptcy while being a doctor.

Today, he's in his midfifties and still struggling to fight his way out of debt. Even after the decades he's invested in his profession, he has insufficient retirement savings and nothing set to the side. He continues to work relentlessly to make ends meet. Unfortunately, his story is like so many others', proving that professionals can and do fail—even doctors.

Myth #4: Running a Business Shouldn't Take Much of Your Time

Like most things in life, being a successful business owner requires time. However, there appears to be a misconception floating about out there that it doesn't or maybe shouldn't. This final myth can set any entrepreneur up for failure because running a business isn't a side hustle you can tackle in your spare time. Building and growing a business requires a hefty amount of time because there are many facets of it that need your focus and attention.

For instance, your employees will be the heart and soul of your success. Taking time to interview, vet, and select the right candidates won't happen overnight.

Also, if you attempt to run your practice during your "spare time," you'll fail to effectively learn where your competitors stand. You may not do a decent job of keeping up with what you're doing better than them or what they're doing better than you. You won't know what improvements need to be made. In the end, you won't have a business—you'll just have a half-baked operation that's barely had a chance to lift its feet off the ground before it finally collapses.

To achieve success you have to make sure you work *on* your business, not just *in* it. This requires tons of time and focus, so that's what you must prepare to give.

DON'T FALL PREY TO THE MYTHS: DEVELOP THE SMALL BUSINESSPERSON IN YOU

The four big myths are easy to get swept into. However, once you're aware of them and take the right precautions, they're just as easily avoidable. To be a successful physician entrepreneur, you have to stop yourself from buying into these lies. Once you do that, it's time to drop the mind-set of a physician and adopt the mind-set of a small businessperson. This requires drastically shifting the way you think, which you can accomplish in many different ways.

Think Like a Businessperson, Not a Medical Professional

When I started my business, it was all about me. I was working on patients, running the front desk, keeping track of the books, and trying to pull the maximum number of customers through my doors. Later I realized what I was doing wasn't called running a business; it was called running a one-man show. My business wasn't a business at all. It was a glorified version of me doing my job that I simply tacked the label of "running a business" on because I didn't know better. I had no team. I had no procedures. All I had was myself, and I was doing it all. That's not the definition of a business by any standard. A business is about building a team; expanding that team; putting systems, policies, and people in place; putting the right people in the right places; and creating a robust culture. Ultimately if you do all those things, you'll have a turnkey operation that relies less on you and more on your team. That's a business.

Put the right people in the right places, show up, and watch the magic begin.

Dr. Edwin Williams

Unfortunately, when those components aren't in place, you don't have a business. This is an amateur mistake physicians make all the time, especially those in aesthetic medicine. They create a practice that runs completely off of one doctor. They don't understand that a business is defined as something that can hold value and be sold, and in having one doctor run the show, they hold an entity that has neither one of those characteristics.

When you transform your mind-set to think like a business owner and not a medical professional, you'll focus more on building a team and less on performing the most transactions. Eventually, this will lead you to better productivity, clarity, and peace of mind, which are some of the benefits of running your own practice.

But what happens if you don't know the first thing about what it means to think like a businessperson? That's a valid concern that brings us to our next key point.

Become a Student of Business

When I set foot out of medical school, one of the skills I possessed was knowing how to practice frugality. That skill alone helped me survive as a physician entrepreneur for about the first ten years. However, after that, I realized I was missing a key element in propelling my practice to that next level. I was working like crazy, trying to be everywhere at once, and feeling completely depleted of energy at the end of the workday.

Matters only continued spiraling out of control until one day my current chief operating officer intervened, pulling me to the side just as I was flitting off to the next patient. "We need to do something. You need a partner. You can't continue working like this," she warned me.

That's when I knew something had to give. That's also when I decided on what I had to do next to see a positive change in the way we were running our operations: I had to become a student of business.

If you don't take care of your business, it won't take care of you.
Dr. Edwin Williams

Although I knew how to stretch a dollar to the max, I would be the first to admit that I didn't know the first thing about drumming up a profit-and-loss sheet or building an effective work culture.

Initially in my venture to become a student of business, I applied and got accepted into an executive master of business administration program, but I nixed that idea soon after when I realized that the very thought of spending hours away from my family rubbed me the wrong way. One day, after a lot of internal struggle, I took a deep breath and peered in the mirror. "Come on, Williams," I muttered. "You're no dummy. Figure this out."

Immediately, I set to work with a game plan brewing in my mind. I got started, plucking a syllabus from one of the MBA programs I had briefly considered. On it were a range of topics covering every subject from marketing to accounting and strategic planning. My strategy was to read as many books as I possibly could on all of the many topics on the syllabus. I listened to books on tape about accounting. I devoured aisles and aisles of business books at the local bookstore. I even got the *Harvard Business Review* on CD and listened to it on the way to work for several years until the concepts made sense from repetition and I gained clarity.

Even today, I haven't stopped learning. Nowadays, however, instead of CDs, I tune into podcasts. In fact, I have my own podcast where I share a regular stream of knowledge on running your own practice. (If you're interested, you can listen in at dredwinwilliams. com.) The insight I share on my podcast has been gleaned both from my own experiences as well as trainings and books I myself have learned from.

In my spare time, I also browse the self-help aisles of libraries, which are stocked with wonderful works on business.

Whichever method of instruction most suits you is irrelevant. The key is to remain open minded and coachable. Acknowledge that being intelligent enough to become a physician doesn't necessarily qualify you to run a business. Reading balance sheets, deciphering profit-loss statements, and learning the art of implementing strategic planning sessions and performing a SWOT (strengths, weaknesses, opportunities, and threats) analysis are a must and should be part of your daily vernacular.

To learn these skills, you must seek professional help—from books, mentors, or someplace else. If being a physician and relying on someone else to teach you the tricks of the trade in running a business puts you off or embarrasses you, consider this: even Tiger Woods, arguably one of the world's greatest golfers, has a coach. So why not you?

The most liberating part about learning is that over time you'll have less and less to learn because several concepts will repetitively be fed to you through multiple experts. This repetition not only helps lend validity to the knowledge you're absorbing but also helps you feel a greater sense of confidence and clarity in knowing you're heeding sound advice since several industry-top professionals are delivering it.

Take Jack Welch, author of *Winning*, for example. He famously said that you should anticipate about 10 percent turnover on your team. If you're not seeing that level of turnover, you're being too easy as a boss, and if you see more than that, you haven't successfully built a team.

Welch was also popular for preaching that companies should be slow to hire and quick to fire. Today, this saying is prevalently practiced across different industries. It's not unusual for leadership to "work date" a potential employee for several months before they extend a permanent placement offer.

As you're reading and learning from the experts, go beyond simply reading to taking action. Learn and then implement what've you learned because simply learning isn't good enough. To see results, you must execute upon your knowledge.

Unfortunately, many rising entrepreneurs don't bother becoming students of business. Or if they do, they fail to apply their newfound wisdom, becoming no more than cogs running in a wheel—bringing in money from one hand and spending it with the other.

However, if you apply your learnings, the magic of becoming a student can prove transformational, and the results you'll see will be outstanding, saving you both money and time.

People always think time is money. Time isn't money. Time is life.

Dr. Edwin Williams

Spend with Caution

All my life I'd grown up seeing my parents spend money only on necessities—never desires. Today, I am grateful for that experience because growing up around them, I adopted this mind-set too.

For instance, when having to choose between attending an in-state or out-of-state college for medical school, I chose an in-state one because it was more affordable. When I had to select between a pricey car and an economical one post-med-school graduation, I chose a fifteen-year-old one with 175,000 miles on it and a marginal monthly payment.

These decisions didn't require concentrated effort—they came naturally to me because of my upbringing. Dad was known for thinking two steps ahead, spending one cent and saving ten. As it turned out, being trained in this manner early on is what made me a more prudent risk-taker and a much better businessperson than if I'd conducted myself like most physicians, who were confident they'd make at least $200,000 a year and were eager to spend it all at their will. Eventually, many of these people would be the same ones to graduate med school and launch a practice only to use it as a personal piggy bank.

The business mind-set I'd adopted from my parents made me different. When I graduated I still had the walk and talk of a scrapper—I was accustomed to living well within my means after years of surviving with my parents through the highs and lows of business. I never overleveraged my earnings, which put me in an ideal position to take on a healthy level of risk when it came time to launch my practice and build out a facility. I had no financial backing other than my personal savings and a promising revenue stream. Even when it came to purchasing equipment, I refused to walk into a bank and finance it outright. I paid for a large amount through my savings, choosing to finance only a small outstanding balance.

I've found that to be a successful physician entrepreneur, you must embrace this critical step: get out of the mind-set of guaranteed success and step into the mind-set of an uncertain tomorrow.

> # Just because you're a physician doesn't mean you're entitled to a lavish lifestyle; you must pay your dues before you see the returns.
> **Dr. Edwin Williams**

Essentially, this means you must spend within your limits and place a cap on the number of guilty pleasures you indulge in. That's not to say you should turn into a miser. It simply means you should pick and choose select luxuries—not make your entire existence into one giant guilty pleasure. Having guilty pleasures is normal, healthy, and perfectly acceptable within limits. I have a few of my own. For instance, I love flying, which is why I've invested in a few planes.

I also relish vacations with my family and their significant others. Every year, we go on a nice getaway. We rent a big place in the mountains and take an entire week to ski, eat well, shop, and pamper ourselves. I pick up the tab for family and guests—doing so brings me joy.

> # The happiest people on earth aren't those who focus on material things. They are the ones who focus on experiences and spending time with others.
>
> **Dr. Edwin Williams**

However, in other aspects of my life, I draw the purse strings tighter because I know splurging on everything is not healthy, prudent, or practical. For instance, I may love planes and own a few, but I'm also the same person who happily drives a car with 150,000 miles on it. I pick and choose my indulgences.

This level of discipline gives you a balanced dose of financial freedom—both personally and professionally from a risk standpoint.

Unfortunately, in our line of work, there's a temptation to keep up with the Joneses. Everyone feels they should have the best of everything and better than everyone else. However, in that race no one gets ahead; no one wins. The truth is winning shouldn't be the end goal. The end goal, the true mind-set, should be to grow your practice and make it attractive enough so you can sell at any moment. In chapter 4, we'll delve deeper into how you can set up your business this way. But before we do that, we need to cover another integral point—leadership—which is what we'll discuss in the next chapter.

KEY TAKEAWAYS

→ Physicians are fed four big myths:
  ▷ Education is your biggest asset.
  ▷ Businesses are launched by people who have entrepreneurial skills.
  ▷ Professionals don't fail.
  ▷ You can run a business in your spare time.

→ These myths are the reasons why many physicians fall into the trappings of failure.

→ There are ways to avoid buying into these myths by shifting your mind-set:
  ▷ Think like a businessperson, not a medical professional.
  ▷ Become a student of business.
  ▷ Spend with caution.

→ Ultimately, these mind-set shifts will help you get your thoughts in the place they really should be: thinking about how you can grow your business in a way that it could sell for a lucrative penny at any given point.

CHAPTER 3

THE LEADERSHIP IMPERATIVE

A t some point, you've probably flown Southwest Airlines. If not, you've likely heard of them or the company's former CEO Herb Kelleher.

Southwest has what I'd call a palpable culture (a really important topic but for another chapter). There used to be a time, about ten years ago, when most of its competitor airlines would snigger behind its back. Ironically, those were the very airlines losing fistfuls of customers and money while Southwest was touting incredible gains and a jovial staff.

Delta was among the losers. I recall boarding a Delta flight to San Diego around this time frame and landing a seat next to an elderly woman of about seventy. The flight captain had just announced takeoff. While everyone around us was already seated and buckled, this woman was visibly struggling to heave her carry-on into the overhead bin.

I glanced around and noted the flight attendants were already buckled in, too, looking on as impatient spectators at this woman. Not one of them rose to offer assistance. Instead, they appeared to be telepathically urging her, "Hurry up so we can take off, lady!"

"Ma'am, would you like some help?" I offered, sensing her exasperation.

She looked at me with an expression of complete relief and gratitude. "Yes, please," she replied. Then she leaned in and said, "I'm just afraid if I don't hurry, I'll get yelled at, you see?"

For a customer to fear being publicly embarrassed for something so easily resolvable, to me, was ridiculous. However, the woman's sentiments spoke volumes of Delta's reputation in the industry.

When you contemplate the differences between these two airline giants, Delta and Southwest, you might wonder what it is that makes one more successful than the other. Some might argue it's the customer service. Undoubtedly that has something to do with it, but it's much deeper than that. All the facets of a company weigh heavily on one key player regardless of industry: the leader. The CEO.

Southwest was performing incredibly. It had a leader who was promoting a healthy culture and was invested in the company, its employees, and its customers.

Delta wasn't.

Fast-forward to 2016 when Delta hired a new CEO by the name of Ed Bastian. Sometime that year, I took my chances, booking and boarding another Delta flight. Immediately, I could see signs of differences from my previous experience. When we deplaned, the pilots stood near the exit, smiling and thanking us for choosing their airline. The staff appeared more patient and friendly, too—even happy.

Delta's most recent performance report was released in early 2019, and the company placed number one in the industry. Their culture is palpable to the point that, today, Delta is my preferred airline of choice.

This may all seem completely irrelevant to being a physician entrepreneur and running a successful practice, but I assure you it's not. These anecdotes prove a point: any business, including practices, must learn to leverage the skill of leadership—and that leadership must come from you.

THE DIFFERENCE BETWEEN MANAGERS AND LEADERS

Leadership is an integral skill that's largely absent from school curricula, yet it plays a huge role in your success as an aspiring physician entrepreneur.

Unfortunately, people toss the term *leadership* around fairly loosely. I hear it all the time: "She's a great leader" or "We need a leader to fill this role" or "I'm a leader in my organization."

The term *leader*, however, wields a lot more power than most give it credit for. In reality, there's a distinct difference between a manager and a leader.

A great manager can put each person on the correct seat of the bus, so to speak, and support them. They'll be cognizant about making sure employees are in the right role and focus time on discovering each employee's strengths and weaknesses. Years ago, the focus then shifted on *developing* identified weaknesses into strengths. Today, however, managers are more about leveraging people's strengths and talents while guiding them toward *managing* their weaknesses.

Now take leadership. It works completely differently. If I were tasked to apply just a single word to describe it, it would be this: influence. Because above all else, leadership is simply the ability to influence people, their behaviors, their actions, and their sentiments.

Leaders are more effective than managers because the respect and admiration they command drives people to care about them, be loyal to them, and follow them.

To put it simply, the difference between managing people and leading them is clear: managers fulfill a job description, a responsibility. Leaders empower, motivate, inspire, and create magic in the workplace.

So which is easier? Being a manager or a leader?

You might guess that being a leader is tough, but being a manager is actually the more challenging of the two. Managers must constantly attempt to persuade, encourage, and mold people into what they need them to be, but effective leaders naturally inspire people to follow them and do the right thing with minimal effort.

That's why leaders, not managers, get paid the big bucks. Because an extraordinary leader makes a huge impact on their staff, employees, company and, ultimately, its bottom line—all through influence.

PHYSICIANS AS LEADERS

To have a successful business, you must strive to be a successful leader. You might argue that running a practice is not the same as running a business, so the principle of leadership doesn't apply. However, your practice is still a type of business, and a business runs best based on the same basic principles regardless of how many employees it has, where it's located, or which industry it's a part of.

That being said, I will admit that running a physician practice is a very *unique* business.

For instance, I have friends who are presidents and CEOs of their own companies. Their ultimate job is to function as a leader—

every day—assuming the roles and responsibilities a leader typically does.

Meanwhile, physicians are stuck in a catch-22 because if they spend the majority of their time being leaders, there's no one left to tend to patients.

As a surgeon myself, I don't have the luxury of sitting in my office eight hours a day to focus on leading. I'm required to be out there, scrubs on, gloves at the ready, performing surgery.

At the same time, while I'm doing that, someone has to be out there to run the operations side of the business—practices can't be successful on just operations or practice alone. Both aspects have to be balanced for the practice to realize success.

That's what makes running your own practice a bit tricky. Many physicians attempt to run the business in their "spare time," which is not feasible or wise, as we've previously discussed.

However, there is a way around this, and the solution is pretty simple: hire an exceptional leader and those who have potential to become leaders as you continue to build your leadership pipeline. Let me reiterate that this isn't the same as hiring a manager. Our businesses have five managers, all of whom have great leadership potential and skills because I am fanatical about developing leaders. Then I give them leadership training and hold them accountable, and you will watch the cream float to the top. The best leaders continue to step up and put it to the bottom line.

An effective leader will step in when you can't and run the operations side of your business. Then once you're through donning your white coat, you can step back into leadership.

The other rationale behind hiring a leader is this: the more leaders you're around, the greater a leader you yourself become. Good leaders attract better leaders.

It may sound simple enough: you hire someone to lead, and you lead when you're able. However, for many physicians, it's not quite so easy. They feel at odds with themselves because they can't wrap their minds around the thought of spending all that time and money toiling away at med school only to step into running a business, of all things. Others simply aren't interested in the prospect of understanding operations and management over doing what they most enjoy: medical practice.

However, if there's only one thing you take from this chapter, let it be this: leadership is imperative—in any business or practice. It's simply a nonnegotiable.

HOW TO BE A GREAT LEADER

A good friend of mine ran a successful software company that contracted with many popular medical practices across the nation. In conversation one day, he asked, "Want to know what I've noticed? The most successful practices I see, whether they have three people or ten, all have one thing in common."

"What's that?" I asked, my curiosity piquing.

"They all have one benevolent dictator physician. One leader."

But what makes a great leader and how can you learn to be one? Before you understand the answer to that question, we should first touch on what exactly it is a leader does.

Responsibilities of a Leader

Herb Kelleher used to say that leaders, whether they're the CEO of a company or the leader of a particular group, have three primary roles. The first is to create the company's vision. If your staff doesn't know where you're headed, you can't expect them to follow you there.

That's why establishing and vocalizing a vision is paramount.

The second responsibility Kelleher outlined was culture. (We won't touch on that just yet because it's worthy of its own chapter and has one later in this book.)

Finally, leaders must take initiative to explain how the company makes money. Although doing this might feel redundant or like you're stating the obvious to employees, it's an important task and one that's often overlooked. You're a business. And although you may expect your employees to know what makes that business tick, sometimes it's not so obvious. Or even if it is, hearing it from the leader may unveil new insight or discoveries for your staff and have a greater impact on their output. Staff need to understand what needs to happen for the company to make money, for it to turn a profit. They need to know that when those things happen, they're afforded greater job security, and that when they don't, the converse occurs.

→ You're a business. And although you may expect your employees to know what makes that business tick, sometimes it's not so obvious.

Southwest articulated its revenue-generating story to staff in a simple way: "Wheels Up." Essentially, they mean to say, "We make money every time the wheels of our planes lift up." The airline's staff is familiar with its story—it's a fact that's evident in how fast their planes board and take off.

A few years ago, for instance, I was at the airport, about to get on a return flight home from Miami. On the way to the restroom, I noticed a Southwest plane pulling into the gate. When I returned not fifteen minutes later, the plane was pulling out.

Staff coming together as a unified team can make this possible; it just proves what influence great leadership can have.

Now that we know the responsibilities of a great leader, let's delve a little deeper into some attributes phenomenal leaders share along with some supporting evidence of why leadership is integral.

The Common Attributes of Great Leaders

Jim Collins, a Stanford PhD (doctor of philosophy) professor, wrote a book called *Good to Great* in which he shares his discoveries about publicly traded companies that beat the S&P (Standard & Poor's) consistently for more than fifteen years.

He chose fifteen years as his benchmark because, typically, CEOs in publicly traded companies don't stick around for more than ten years. Studying a company over fifteen years gave a better snapshot of those who made it through at least a few CEOs, validating that the current ones were successful in their own right—not riding off the success or coattails of a previous strong leader.

➜ **Often when I mentor physicians, I offer up the same warning: if you're overexpensing or writing off things you shouldn't be, don't for an instant think your bookkeeper doesn't know.**

When Collins data mined to unveil the secrets behind each CEO's success, he discovered several attributes these leaders shared, proving that great leaders create successful businesses.

First, they possessed impeccable integrity. This is a particularly important trait for obvious reasons—people won't willingly follow someone they don't trust. That almost all of these leaders exhibited this quality validates that it's integral to any leader's—and their company's—success.

Often when I mentor physicians, I offer up the same warning: if you're overexpensing or writing off things you shouldn't be, don't for an instant think your bookkeeper doesn't know. Or if you're speaking poorly about one of your team members to another one, understand that you're damaging your integrity because undoubtedly the person you speak poorly to will question whether they can trust what you say about them behind their back. Do the right thing always, even when you think no one is watching.

The second attribute Collins discovered was the attribute of compassion and taking a genuine interest in others on the team. Before we delve too deep into this one, let's do a quick exercise.

First, think about a leader figure in your life (someone other than a parent) whom you disliked. Write down words to describe that person. This should be someone you knew personally enough to describe.

What adjectives did you use?

Disinterested? Harsh? Mean? A bully? It shouldn't surprise you then that these are the very antonyms of a good leader.

Now repeat the same exercise, but this time think of an amazing leader who's made a lasting impact on you. Write down the attribute you most appreciated about this person. Again, think of someone you knew personally, not a celebrity or politician you've read about.

Almost everyone who does this exercise chooses the same attribute: they describe this person as being caring or compassionate. If you reflect back on the leader you thought of, you'll likely notice that they took a moment to slow down and look you in the eye.

If they were truly extraordinary, they likely also possessed the third and final attribute Collins discovered in most great leaders:

being an active listener—some, with their hearts. These types of leaders take a genuine interest in people.

I remember learning this lesson the hard way.

There was once a nurse who worked with us and was being bullied by another nurse. I didn't know of this at the time, and ultimately, the victim grew tired and resigned. During her exit interview with my chief operating officer, she explained her reasons for leaving. Then she finished off by saying, "Besides, I don't know if Dr. Williams even really likes me or cares that I'm here."

I was crushed. I hadn't known that she'd thought that, but in hindsight, I understood why she would. Anytime I was at work, I was occupied with a patient, busy on my laptop, or distracted reviewing the schedule. In other words, I was doing everything except listening and giving consideration to the people who helped my business thrive: my employees. The last item on my agenda at any given time was being a leader. However, the feedback received through this incident taught me an important lesson. It taught me to slow down and take genuine interest. It taught me that I needed to stop every now and again and ask people about them, about their families, about life. I needed to connect with them as people—because that's who we all are.

The great news about leadership is that contrary to what some may believe, great leaders aren't born; they're created. This means that being a great leader is very much within your reach if you wish it to be.

Ways to Sharpen Your Leadership Skills

In my decades of mentoring doctors, the one thing I can say with certainty is that about 30–40 percent of them are not coachable because of one reason and one reason only: ego.

Ego is probably one of the most destructive qualities anyone, especially those aspiring to be leaders, can have. In fact, in Collins's book *Good to Great*, he distinguishes the best leaders (or as he calls them, level-five leaders) from the rest by the absence of that single vice: ego.

To become an effective leader, the first step is to toss your ego. That means making things about others, not you—whether victory or defeat. Good leaders let their team carry the victory, shine with success, and win the credit; they're not out to score gold stars themselves, receive a pat on the back, or win kudos. On the other hand, they take responsibility for the team's defeat instead of passing blame on the team or growing defensive.

Next, you must be coachable and open to learning. For me, that receptiveness comes in the form of being a student to good leaders by observing their attributes, mannerisms, thoughts, and idiosyncrasies.

Another great trait leaders share is they trust people but also respectfully hold them accountable. Train your staff, give them the resources they need to succeed, but also, let them fail. If you don't make room for failure, you'll paralyze your staff. If you're constantly hovering over them, dictating their every move, they'll never learn how to handle situations on their own. Permit them to make their own mistakes, whether it's mis-scheduling or giving the wrong information to someone. Then take a moment to debrief later in the day so you can coach, but do so with respect.

Finally, one way to ensure you're sharpening your leadership skills is by overcoming complacency. A great leader never grows complacent. In leadership, there's simply no room for it.

> I don't know what success is. But the last hurdle to success, whatever that is, is complacency.

Dr. Edwin Williams

KEY TAKEAWAYS

→ Managers fill a job description while leaders empower, motivate, and inspire.

→ Practice great leadership by observing other great leaders.

→ Learn to have compassion with employees, and treat them as humans first, employees last.

→ The responsibilities of a leader include
   ▷ creating a company vision,
   ▷ fostering a company culture, and
   ▷ explaining to employees how the company makes money.

→ The attributes of a great leader include
   ▷ integrity,
   ▷ compassion, and
   ▷ great listening skills.

CHAPTER 4

SYSTEMS, POLICIES, PROCEDURES, AND DEVELOPING A CULTURE OF WINNING AND ACCOUNTABILITY

I read a story in *The E-Myth Revisited*, by Michael Gerber, that's been etched in my mind ever since. It was an anecdote about a lady named Sarah. Sarah loved to bake—it was her passion. In fact, she was so fond of baking that one day, she decided to open her own bakery. For a while, Sarah found herself knee-deep in struggles. She was investing eighty hours a week in her business and had no time for anything else. A few years pass, and Sarah is finally the owner of a successful bakery that's generating revenue, garnering attention, and receiving praise.

Despite these successes, Sarah realizes that something's still off. Instead of loving what she does, she dreads it because she's drained.

She's the baker and also the washer, bookkeeper, manager, and everything else. The problem is, although she's a successful baker, what she hasn't been successful at is creating a business through implementing the right systems. And without these systems, her business isn't scalable. In other words, what she has is a job, not a business.

This anecdote illustrates our next key topic: the significance of systems, policies, and procedures in a small business. Once you adjust your mind-set, like we discussed in chapter 2, the next step is to employ the right systems, policies, and procedures.

When you order fries at any McDonald's, you get the same crispy, salty flavor delivered in a standard paper sleeve with the brand's famous golden arches. In essence, what you're witnessing is a turnkey operation in action. Meticulous systems, policies, and procedures are what enable McDonald's to deliver a consistent, uniform experience across its franchise—regardless of location. A robust system is also what empowers it to sell its stores at top dollar. That's the power of systems.

The same holds true for practices. Put systems in place—from operations to accounting to legal—and watch how they transform your business.

THE IMPORTANCE OF SYSTEMS

There once was an oral surgeon who was part of a four-person practice. The practice was performing well, so the owning surgeons decided to invite him on board as a partner, offering him buy-in and equity in the practice.

Thrilled, the surgeon began his due diligence. He solicited the advice of his attorney and accountant. Both parties took care to review the business and returned with the same concern: the practice had no systems—legal or accounting—in place. They asked the oral surgeon a question he struggled to answer: "With no operations evident, what exactly are you buying?"

Concerned, the surgeon left the practice and went across town, where he joined the competition. In the end, the practice lost a rock-star surgeon—all because of a lack of policies and systems.

→ **The moral of the story is simple: systems are important.**

The moral of the story is simple: systems are important. They're what help you morph a job into a business and a turnkey operation that's attractive to investors—whether future stakeholders or private investors.

But how can systems be a game changer for your practice, and how can you benefit by leveraging them? That's a topic we'll tackle next.

SOLVING THE PHYSICIAN'S CONUNDRUM

We know physicians are technicians and are rarely ever (like most people) born with the know-how to run a business. They're valued based on their ability to generate revenue or rake in the largest number of surgical cases. Most of the time, you'll find them flitting from one patient to the next in an endless frenzy. For physician entrepreneurs, policies and procedures allow you to resume the continuity of being a technician. They're what empower you to continue your work as a physician with minimal interruptions and setbacks.

Ten or fifteen years ago, it wouldn't have been unusual for one of my managers to approach me seconds before I was entering a room to perform a three-hour surgery and say, "Hey, Dr. Williams, we have problem XYZ." The majority of the time, the grievances weren't anything urgent, which made these interruptions all the more frustrating.

But that's usually the nature of the business for physicians: even when you have your own practice, you're doubling as head honcho and technician. Wearing both hats simultaneously is difficult, if not impossible. That's where systems and policies come into play, helping run the show while you're busy doing what you should be doing—taking care of patients.

Today, several business books and audio trainings later, you'll never see me get approached unless it's an emergency (which, thankfully, is rare) because I have ironclad systems in place. Let's talk about what a strong system actually looks like.

EXAMPLES OF SMART SYSTEMS

There was once this charming little hotel in Carmel, California, where a man once stayed while on business. Upon checking in, he was given an intake form to complete, which asked him several questions about his personal preferences: his favorite flavor of coffee, his preferred coffee shop, which newspapers he subscribed to, and so on. Once his trip drew to a close, he flew back home, only to return to that same hotel several years later. When he awoke the first morning of his stay, the staff delivered his favorite Starbucks latte. At the threshold, he found the *Wall Street Journal*, his newspaper of choice. The man was utterly amazed. He had completely forgotten the form he'd filled out all those years ago—and he was oblivious to the fact that an intelligent system had stored all those details so they could be used again in the future.

Experiences like these wow customers—and they're possible thanks to smart systems.

If you have systems in place for 20 percent of the things that drive 80 percent of your business and you insist on your team following them 100 percent of the time, you win.

Dr. Edwin Williams

For physicians, smart systems serve a different purpose, of course.

At our practice, a patient who is seen in consultation has a pre-consult with one of our patient concierges (PCs), then sees the doctor and the PC, and finishes with the PC in postconsult where fees are discussed and, hopefully, surgery is booked.

Several years ago we decided to tape these consults for quality and learning purposes since we had separate employees conducting each one. The recordings revealed that much of the same information was repeatedly being fed to potential patients because staff members weren't aware of which topics their peers had already covered in previous consults. Essentially, we were wasting the patient's time. Further observations taught us that, on average, patients only tuned in for the first forty minutes or so, after which their attention waned.

Using this information, we implemented an intelligent system. We divided the information that needed to be covered into segments, allotting each piece to be discussed either during preconsult, consultation, or postconsult. Then we took it a step further and created a playbook, which we made mandatory for the team to follow.

With the implementation of this playbook, our process today works much more seamlessly and efficiently for both us and our patients. It's also boosted our conversion rate for each consult by about 10–15 percent depending on the procedure.

That's exactly the aim and intention of systems: to make processes more automated and seamless. The same power that systems wield in transforming your business, policies hold too.

THE SIGNIFICANCE OF POLICIES

Policies allow you to make decisions on the spot. They lay a ground-work of established rules everyone must follow.

One of the policies at our practice is that all nonurgent communications between team members must be conducted either through email or voicemail. The logic behind this rule might be questioned, but the policy was created, like most others, because of events that made it necessary for it to exist. It started a number of years ago when I hired a capable bookkeeper. Although she seemed a fantastic fit for the job, had an office sectioned off from the rest of the staff, and was solely focused on bookkeeping, she could never complete her work on time. We soon identified the issue: people were constantly loitering around her office to pop in with questions, congregate, and even socialize. Meanwhile, the bookkeeper didn't have the willpower to refuse their company; it was no wonder she couldn't complete her work.

To help her out, we introduced office hours for two hours at the end of the business day when staff could meet with her using a sign-up sheet so she could spend the core of her workday actually focused on bookkeeping. After many conversations and warnings encouraging her to remain focused, we were left with no choice but to let her go and enforce this policy.

Another policy we've implemented is a copycat of one the Ritz-Carlton adopted. The Ritz, as everyone knows, is famous for its stellar reputation with customer service. To embrace a customer-first approach, they allot $2,000 to each member of their team, and the money can be spent at that member's discretion to improve a customer's experience. Say, for instance, a customer gets worked up about missing room service and a team member learns it's their spouse's birthday. He can use his discretionary funds to treat the couple to a complimentary spa day to make up for the inconvenience.

Piggybacking off this policy, our practice allots employees $1,000 of discretionary funds to satisfy our patients. We've found this to be much more effective than a patient requesting compensation for a subpar experience and then waiting for staff to seek approval or check the guidelines on a policy. Frankly, when a customer is upset, the last thing they want is to hear you ramble about some policy or rule book you need to consult. They much more appreciate empowered associates who can empathize with them and take action independently to make wrongs right.

When designing policies, ask yourself which repetitive distractions or roadblocks you encounter daily. Likely, a policy or a system could resolve the issue, saving you time, reducing frustrations, and wowing your customers.

Although it'd be wonderful to say that policies and systems can come to the rescue each and every time, that's simply not true. These tools can't solve for every single scenario you'll ever see.

> # The problem with systematizing everything is that you then do not give people the discretion to use their brains to make decisions—you must let them fail.
>
> Dr. Edwin Williams

There isn't a binder big enough in the world to fit all the systems and policies for every single circumstance that might crop up. That's where culture comes into play.

WHERE SYSTEMS AND POLICIES MEET COMPANY CULTURE

Like leadership, culture is another word that's tossed around loosely. However, it's much greater than something you simply define on a sheet of paper or scrawl on your break room walls. Culture is the living, breathing essence of your business. It's what's going on when no one is looking. Culture is what allows your team to make decisions in a split second when management or rule books aren't there to guide you toward what's right.

I remember we once had a patient who'd had a Mohs procedure performed and then showed up in our office unannounced. While the Mohs surgeon had successfully removed the tumor, he'd left a gaping, horrific hole on her face, and somehow we never received the call that he was sending the patient over for a plastic repair. The woman walked into our office distressed and upset—she didn't have an appointment. An essential part of our culture is that customers always come first when they're in need, and our staff knows this. So the moment the woman walked through the doors, even lacking an appointment, our front desk staff didn't falter. They didn't have to reference a policy book or approach management because patients always come first. Our culture told them everything they needed to make a split-second decision. "Come on in," they told the patient. "We'll take care of you in just a moment."

It's inaccurate to say that culture is derived from just one aspect of your business; many factors will shape your company culture.

FACTORS THAT INFLUENCE CULTURE

Four key components will typically mold your culture: (1) communication, (2) training, (3) a system of accountability, and (4) competition. Several subcategories may also fall under these primary segments and influence your organizational ambiance. Leverage each of these components in different ways to create a stellar culture for your practice.

Communication

Culture is influenced by the communication style you opt for with both clients and staff. I'll elaborate by touching on the various ways in which you might communicate with staff, using some examples we employ at my practice.

Huddles

Each morning, our staff gathers around for a ten- to twelve-minute morning huddle as soon as we arrive. The first few minutes, we focus on highlighting our wins from the previous day and summarizing our best and worst moments.

The next three to five minutes are spent mapping out the day's appointments and tasks.

In the final three to four minutes, we discuss challenges, doing a round-robin to ensure everyone gets a chance to speak.

These huddles enforce a culture of effective communication, but their purpose runs much deeper.

Once, a woman who came to us for a consultation brought several of her grandchildren along for the visit. By the time her turn arrived, the grandkids were running wild, getting rowdy, impatient, and disruptive. You could see the anxiousness etched on their grandmother's face as she hesitated to be seen for her consult. One of our staff sensed her apprehension and immediately got to work, rounding up the grandchildren and taking them into another room that she filled with toys. She stayed there, playing with them until the grandmother was finally through with her appointment.

The next morning in our huddle, the staff member was recognized with a gift card in appreciation of her outstanding job in upholding our culture and putting our client at ease. So daily huddles for us serve multiple purposes—they're great for day-to-day communicating but also to reinforce positive messages through positive action.

Performance Evaluations

Another time to establish culture through communication is during performance reviews. Some companies may choose to perform regular evaluations. At our practice, we feel the word *evaluation* carries a negative connotation, so we opt to conduct one-on-one *coaching* sessions (more on these a bit later) where we offer candid feedback on how well each member is living up to our company's credo and motto, both of which are integral to fostering a strong culture.

Our motto, for instance, is "We take care of each other and you."

Several years ago, a sweet woman who worked our front desk was on her way to work when her tires went flat about ten miles north of the office. "I'm sorry," she told us, "but I'm going to be late coming in." One of our managers, who'd heard she was stranded, jumped into her own car and headed out to the employee. When she arrived, she took control of the situation, using her AAA (American Automobile Association) membership to call a tow service. She paid for everything. Not once did that manager approach me to see if it was okay for her to leave work and help the employee. She knew her actions were acceptable because taking care of each other is part of our culture.

Priorities aren't what you say; they're what you do.

Dr. Edwin Williams

During performance evaluations, we identify not only how well the employee is performing in their job but also how well they're embracing our culture. When your culture is strong, your company is strong. And when your company is strong, your patients sense it.

Managers' Meetings

Just like it's important for you to communicate with your staff, it's important for you communicate with managers and leaders too. Every month, our practice conducts a managers' meeting where we meet as a group and discuss a preset agenda for ninety minutes. During these meetings, our focus, again, is to keep the lines of communication open. We discuss our wins and strategies and what's going on with the business, new hires, employees, and so on. Ultimately, these meetings help us communicate with each other to ensure we're all on the same page and treading in the same direction.

Training

Before we focus on how to train your staff so they embrace and reflect your company culture, let's take a step back and talk about how to first hire the right people to represent that culture.

Hiring

Larry Bossidy, the former CEO of Honeywell, wrote a book called *Execution: The Discipline of Getting Things Done.* In this work, he challenges popular beliefs by saying that contrary to what most people think, the CEO's number one job isn't just to have a strong strategy and keen understanding of the market. Fifty percent of the job is about who they hire and who they fire. According to Bossidy, these actions single-handedly set the tone for the entire organization.

At our practice, we have a strict interview process that transpires primarily through the phone. If a potential hire aces the phone interview, only then are they invited to come in for an in-person interview. However, we don't wait until the in-person interview to educate applicants about who we are. Often, you'll hear our interviewing managers saying to candidates, "We're a team here, and one of our rules is that we never talk about each other."

In our organization, talking behind someone's back is grounds for dismissal because working together as a team and not against each other is a part of our culture. (Along those lines, however, if an employee has an issue with someone on the team, management practices an open-door policy and employees are always welcome to come speak with us.)

Once we establish our culture during the early interview stage and the candidate passes the in-person interview, we move on to background checks. This is where we contact references to ask them questions about the candidate to gauge their personality. Typical questions might be, "On a scale of one to ten, how would you rate this person as someone you would want on your team?" and "How often have you ever seen this person gossip?"

We've intentionally designed these questions to be open ended because we want to elicit an honest answer from references. Also, the intent behind this grilling is to determine how well the potential new hire stacks up against our culture.

Training on the Job

During the last fifteen to twenty minutes of the ninety-minute managers' meetings I mentioned earlier, I focus on teaching and training. This might be something as simple as reviewing the last two chapters of an inspiring book. Or it may be focusing on some other interesting concept about leadership I stumbled across during personal readings or trainings.

As a practice, we leverage a training resource called Allergan Access. Most businesses don't enroll in Allergan's program, but I find tremendous value in the training and information it provides.

In addition to that, we have a quarterly training for our leaders. In these meetings we do team building and bonding activities to foster relationships among the group and also offer hands-on training to help our leaders become better influencers.

SYSTEMS OF ACCOUNTABILITY

The third integral component of developing a potent company culture is creating a system of accountability. This means holding your staff and company responsible against certain performance metrics. We accomplish this by having structured meetings that follow a specific agenda. We all discuss action items for each thing on the agenda, implement a timeline for the item, and then assign a responsible party for it. The next month, we follow up on the action items to see how we're tracking.

KPIs, or key performance indicators, promote a great system of accountability. Leveraging them, you can track company and employee performance through answers to questions such as "How many consultations have we done?" or "What is our conversion rate?" or "How many Google reviews did we get?"

We also hold our employees to individual performance metrics. For instance, it's not uncommon for me to ask a manager whom they've coached in the past month. A policy at our practice is to hold coaching sessions biannually: once on the anniversary date of the employee's hire and then again six months later.

Our approach to these coachings, as I mentioned earlier, is slightly different than what might take place in your typical evaluation. We maintain a positive, conversational tone and make sure the employee understands that we're having a conversation with them as a member who is part of our team and culture. Coaching conversations might go something like this: "Hey, John. We think you're doing an excellent job. We just wanted to talk to you about the things you're awesome about and maybe some of the things we think you could improve on."

Usually at the end of these ninety-minute coachings, we'll finish off by setting customized goals for each individual for the following six months.

Finally, at the tail end, we ask employees to share their thoughts about their experience by asking questions such as "What's the biggest challenge you face in your job?"

We find that while most employees are hesitant to share struggles during a huddle or group meeting, they're more willing to open up in a one-on-one situation. Sometimes that's because some of the challenges they face are in part caused by another coworker. For instance, in a huddle, an employee is unlikely to say, "Hey, I'm having a tough time getting my charts done because Judy keeps running out the door at 4:00 p.m. every day when she's supposed to be sticking back and helping me."

Our coaching sessions are designed so employees can provide feedback in a secluded, private environment where we express genuine interest in their thoughts.

Studies prove that the majority of people leave jobs not because of pay but because of frustration. However, you won't ever know if your employees are frustrated if you never take the time to listen.

Beyond just a performance improvement mechanism, coachings are designed to detect frustrations and problems proactively while simultaneously empowering us to invest in our relationships with employees.

Contest the Hell out of Everything

The fourth and last element of creating a robust culture is generating healthy competition. People love to win, and when you give them a shot at that, they're likely to give you their all.

> # Build the right culture and everyone from your front desk receptionists to your behind-the-scenes surgeons will be invested in your company and in doing the right thing for it.
>
> Dr. Edwin Williams

For instance, as a reward for outstanding performance, we select top employees and jet them off with us to our national meetings. This brings forth a sense of competition and makes the winners feel appreciated and rewarded for their hard work and efforts.

Now that we know the four elements that contribute to a great company culture, you might still have a tiny question niggling the back of your brain: Why does culture even matter?

THE SIGNIFICANCE OF CULTURE

Culture is important because it translates into higher company morale and more profitability. Tony Hsieh ran a company called

Zappos, which has a robust culture. This brand was so well known for its culture that Hsieh authored a book on the topic called *Delivering Happiness*.

Hsieh's personal experiences with Zappos and the statistics both prove that a strong culture and solid policies cultivate companies that are both more scalable and valuable.

Take Orangetheory Fitness, the relatively new fitness chain, for example. This franchise boasts and breathes incredible culture, which is why they're successful, valuable, and profitable. (Sorry, folks, but I just cannot promote McDonald's here. Their food is disgusting and unhealthy, and while they have incredible systems and policies, I really cannot attest to the culture, which has waxed and waned over the decades. They are currently trying to reinvent themselves.)

Orangetheory Fitness has systems of accountability (one of the cultural drivers we discussed) in place for its members. For example, you can't cancel a class less than twelve hours before the class time. If you do, you are charged an additional penalty. If you don't show up one day, you pay the penalty charge. From a physical fitness standpoint, their heart monitors keep you accountable for your level of exertion, and attendees have no choice but to work hard toward accumulating enough splat points to achieve the desired "afterburn for the next thirty-six hours."

That's why Orangetheory is worth a lot of money—because it has systems and policies embedded in a deep-rooted culture. That's what adds value.

WHY PHYSICIANS FAIL TO IMPLEMENT CULTURE

You understand the significance of culture. You know it's integral for any business. Then why do most physicians fail to instill culture in their practices? In my experience, there are usually four answers to this question.

Ignorance

Most doctors don't know what it truly takes to build a business, including the significance of culture. This relates back to our earlier point about a lack of knowledge leading to a business's demise. Most physicians figure that getting their doctorate is the key to running a practice, so they fail to consider the operations side of things. As we know, business requires a different mind-set and skill set than what the medical curriculum teaches. That's why, for physicians, becoming a student of business is essential.

Lack of Focus on Building a Business

The second factor that prevents physician entrepreneurs from turning their focus to building culture is that most of them simply aren't willing to work on the business side of their practice. They have the mentality that the more cases they take, the more solid their business will grow. However, that type of thinking misses the mark. Because at the end of the day, the practice isn't about you and how many transactions you complete. It's about growing and building a team and developing an operation—something worthy of selling, when the right opportunity arises, either to a partner or an outside entity. This concept could be expanded greatly regarding the corporate practice of medicine, but it is not within the scope of this book.

If you're working solo, you're working a job. You're not building a business, and in turn, you're not building value. When you focus on creating a true business, you'll be able to shift focus to instilling the right culture in your practice.

Hesitancy with Holding People Accountable

Third, most physicians feel discomfort at the prospect of holding employees accountable. Systems can intervene and accomplish this with minimal intervention from you. Most practices I've mentored, unfortunately, have a culture of entitlement. Physicians make good money, so they pay their staff well and are nice to them. They never coach or help them develop. In turn, employees enjoy a generous paycheck for the minimal effort they put forth and end up sticking around forever, to the culture's demise. What you're stuck with are bored employees who foster a gloomy ambiance for your practice and its patients. Trust me, this is true, and for many reasons worthy of an entire discussion, physicians traditionally do a terrible job holding their team accountable in a respectful manner.

Lack of Willingness to Invest in the Team and Self

Finally, physicians aren't willing to invest in their staff. Most of my colleagues complain about their employees. Often, they tell me, "I know you say you have this fantastic team, but I just don't buy it. There are just no good employees out there anymore."

Not only do you have to invest in your team to unearth prized talent and be successful but you also have to continue investing in yourself so you can learn the skills necessary to run a successful practice. If you're not willing to put in the work, you won't see the efforts reflected in your practice or its resulting culture. I personally have spent and continue to spend tens of thousands of dollars and countless hours annually on professional business development and consulting for myself. It has been my experience that most physician entrepreneurs are just unwilling to allocate the time or resources toward this very important effort of running and growing a business.

KEY TAKEAWAYS

→ The best companies have a set of systems, policies, and procedures in place. They also have a palpable culture.

> ▷ Systems help you make processes easier and more simplified.
> ▷ Policies help establish rules so you don't have to micromanage.
> ▷ Culture is your company environment: its values, beliefs, and personality.

→ All three converge to help guide your employees, drive your operations more effortlessly, and make your business valuable.

→ Physicians fail to implement culture for four key reasons:

> ▷ ignorance,
> ▷ lack of focus on building a business,
> ▷ unwillingness to hold people accountable, and
> ▷ lack of willingness to invest in the team and themselves.

CHAPTER 5

THE IMPORTANCE OF STRATEGIC PLANNING

f you're old enough to remember Kodak, you know it's now near extinct. Once the king of camera technology and photography, this brand went belly-up when it turned its nose at the prospect of digitization in the photography industry. Its lack of willingness to embrace and accept the trajectory of the industry ultimately led to its bankruptcy … and its demise.

Shift your attention to Blockbuster, the once-upon-a-time leader in movie and video game rentals, and you encounter an eerily similar story. When Netflix popped up, offering door-to-door delivery for rentals, Blockbuster all but laughed at it. It only took a handful of years for Netflix to gobble up the rental giant whole, leaving it flabbergasted.

Jump to 2002. Yahoo! was set to acquire Google, focusing its efforts on the media aspects of the company and none on its novel search capabilities. Simultaneously, Yahoo! had its sights on Facebook but failed to enter the mobile market. In both these instances, it had targeted the right companies but for the wrong reasons, essentially circling the drain because of its inability to successfully recognize and adopt the right innovations.

Change is important, but changing correctly is integral.

Dr. Edwin Williams

There's an old proverb that goes something like "The only cost more expensive than change is not changing at all." However, to embrace change effectively, you need a strategy. In business, we call this strategic planning, and it's one of the most critical elements to ensure the success of any business.

UNDERSTANDING STRATEGIC PLANNING

Strategic planning is an activity you do as an organization to establish the goals and priorities for your business so you can continue to evolve and adopt changes for the future. These sessions are used to enforce the right energy and ensure all your resources, including employees and stakeholders, are working in sync toward common goals. Done effectively, these sessions produce decisions and actions that shape the future of your organization and the direction it will venture. The best, most effective of these sessions not only establish goals and objectives but also determine how your business will know once it's been successful in achieving them.

Perhaps one of the most important things you should know

about your strategic planning sessions is that everyone in your company, from your frontline receptionists to your most influential leaders, need to be involved in them. Leaving even a single person out could mean missing out on invaluable feedback from a unique perspective.

For instance, at one of our breakout sessions, I asked our staff to think of our weaknesses as a practice. For a moment, the room fell silent as everyone began to think. Finally, one of our front desk staff raised her hand. "We get phone calls all the time for breast augments, but when we quote Dr. Smith's fees, people say, 'Thanks, but Dr. so-and-so across town is much cheaper.' I think we're losing customers to the competition, which is one of our weaknesses."

The staff member who spoke up worked at the receptionist's desk, fielding calls and booking appointments, but her insight was amazing. After a little independent research and verification, my managers and I realized she was absolutely right. Dr. Smith's fees were about $1,000 higher than our average competitor. Until then, I hadn't realized this. My managers hadn't realized it either. Frankly, we probably all would have continued happily in our obliviousness had it not been for the staff member's unique insight into the situation.

At another planning session, we were discussing our nonsurgical Botox™ treatment, which has to be administered every few months and is extremely popular among our patients. One of our receptionists spoke up and presented a valid point that completely changed our outlook on how we scheduled these treatments. "People really want the nonsurgical Botox," she said. "But taking off time from work every few months isn't something that's convenient for them. We should try offering these treatments on the weekends or in the evenings so they're able to get them without taking time off." Again, this advice was brilliant and came from someone who interacted with our customers every day. As a result of this information, we started evening hours two nights a week and one on Saturday mornings just for the nonsurgical treatments.

The bottom line is to make sure you involve your entire team in strategic planning sessions. If you don't, you won't know what valuable insight or information you could be missing out on.

WHY PUT STRATEGY BEHIND PLANNING?

Now that we know what strategic planning is and who should be engaged in these sessions, let's address why it's important. There are several reasons to consider, each of which is valid in its own right.

Keeping Pace with Changing Markets

No industry is ever completely level, meaning there are always ups and downs. The landscape continues to change, technology continues to evolve and expedite that change, and new ideas develop, pushing old ones out of the loop. Without a plan and strategy in place, you won't be able to ride the tides. If you decide to remain oblivious to or ignorant of your surroundings, you only risk getting pulled under the waves. Strategic planning sessions prevent that from happening, allowing you to stay afloat and competitive against the roughest tides so you can conquer any change.

Communication from the Front Line in Your Organization

From my previous anecdotes, you know that all parts of your organization are important—and strategic planning sessions are a great way to draw out the opinions and thoughts of everyone in your practice, including those on your front line. This is made possible through the communication aspect of strategic planning.

For instance, one day at a strategic planning session, I decided to rehash Herb Kelleher's wheels-up story from Southwest. "Who can explain wheels up to me in relationship to our practice?" I asked the group.

One of our patient concierges raised her hand. "Our wheels up, or when we make money, is when our doctors are busy seeing follow-up cosmetic surgical patients back to back."

That statement really blew my mind because this particular PC had been with us for years and her answer *could not have been further from the truth.* But how would she know that if I, as the CEO, had failed to communicate that information to our staff? I'd never taken a moment to explain to them that on the cosmetic surgical side of the practice, we only generate real revenue when we have a cosmetic patient on the table in the operating room.

As we discussed in the chapter on leadership, one of the three primary responsibilities of the leader or CEO of any organization is to effectively teach your team your "wheels up" story. Without this knowledge, they can't help you grow your KPIs. Strategic planning sessions are great opportunities for this dialogue and communication to take place so your staff understand the integral aspects of your business.

Team Building and Buy-In to Your Mission/Vision

When you stick your entire team in a room and make them work toward a common goal, the power is tangible. What starts as a simple question (How do we grow this business?) turns into a magnificent team-building activity. All of a sudden, the room comes alive with ideas, feedback, and thoughts. You're gaining buy-in for your mission/ vision because everyone is involved in the process. And because they're willingly a part of that conversation, they're more inclined to work toward the goals you set as a group. Most importantly, you gain

> → You're gaining buy-in for your mission/ vision because everyone is involved in the process.

loyalty because your employees feel that you appreciate them taking part in that decision-making process—one that not only impacts them but also your entire organization.

Strategic planning helps you realize your objectives. Once you identify what these are, you're able to better track toward executing them. Without strategic planning, you risk spinning your wheels relentlessly with no progress in any positive direction. (Later in this chapter, we'll talk about the different components you should consider when goal setting.)

Why Strategic Planning Is a Challenge for Physicians

I started strategic planning sessions about fifteen years ago, but even today, as I mentor and observe businesses in the aesthetic space, I seldom see them conduct these sessions.

Part of the reason can be traced back to what we talked about earlier as one of the two reasons businesses fail: lack of knowledge. If no one's taught you the importance of or process behind strategic planning, you can't be expected to know any better. Most physicians aren't trained to make time to work on their business. Instead, they're taught to work *in* their business, which is a different undertaking.

The second reason is ego. Physicians usually have a can-do attitude. Their thoughts often venture along the lines of "I'm a doctor. This is my craft—why should I listen to anybody else? I know what I'm doing."

Third, many physicians have a disdain for meetings. Quite honestly, I don't blame them. Often we're forced to sit through many ineffective ones in hospital settings among hospital bureaucrats. We spend hours discussing ideas, action items, and several thoughts that never come to fruition. When the meeting is dismissed, we leave feeling like we've spent too much time discussing a lot and accomplishing nothing. Over time, we begin to think of meetings as an ineffective waste of precious hours we could occupy in much more productive ways. What many physicians don't realize is that meetings can prove effective—if you do them right.

Now that we've discussed what strategic planning is, why you should do it, and the barriers physicians often encounter in adopting a strategic approach, let's get into more detail about how these sessions should play out.

WHEN TO DO STRATEGIC PLANNING

In my opinion, strategic sessions are best planned during seasonal lulls. In the aesthetic business, for instance, some of our largest meetings of the year happen in August or September because that's the slowest time of the year for us. Most people have kids who are preparing to return to school, and several families are finishing up their final vacations of the summer, which is why we see the fewest patients around this time of year. The lower-than-usual volume of patients makes this an ideal time to take a day for strategic planning so we impact the least number of patients through our unavailability. However, whichever time of year you choose for your session, the important thing is to make sure you have maximum attendance from your staff for optimal results.

Length of Strategic Sessions

Most people, as I mentioned earlier, don't leave sufficient time for strategic sessions, which can render them ineffective. Ideally, you should aim to set aside one entire workday for these.

Typically, we close down our entire practice for the day, directing calls to an automated answering system. When I tell fellow colleagues that we do this, I'm usually bombarded with objections. "How can you afford to shut down for an entire day for something like strategic planning?" they ask.

"How can you afford not to?" I ask them in return.

As they say, when you fail to plan, you plan to fail. For me, failure isn't an option, which is why strategic planning is an inbred part of our process and receives the time and attention it requires.

Frequency of Strategic Planning

How often you meet for these sessions depends on the market. In our business we currently find that about once a year is effective at about a 10 percent growth. However, if the market or industry is undergoing rapid change, it's wise to hold more frequent strategic planning sessions.

During my mentoring of professionals, I've noticed that perhaps one of the biggest mistakes they make aside from not allowing ample time for strategic planning sessions is not holding them often enough. The market will clue you in as to the frequency of how regularly you should host these sessions.

For instance, in the med spa market, we're currently seeing significant change. As a result, we're thinking of upping our meetings to twice a year to keep pace with the market shifts. Again, keep an eye on the industry landscape around you to determine the frequency of these meetings.

On that note, it's also important to know that if you have multiple businesses under one umbrella, you should conduct different strategic planning sessions for each. For instance, our medical spa operates differently from our surgical practice, which is different from our hair restoration clinic. These entities each have their own strengths, weaknesses, and goals (topics we'll touch on in just a moment), so it only makes sense that they be analyzed independently in their own sessions.

How to Run an Effective Planning Session

Conducting an impactful strategic planning session entails several things. Typically, if you have a large group, I suggest breaking up into groups of four or five. If you have a much smaller team, you could do groups of two or three.

→ In other words, make every second count, and limit idle chatter.

Our surgical group comprises a large team with three doctors heading the practice. As a result, we have several large clusters in our planning sessions.

Once you've divided up your staff, make sure you time your sessions to keep them effective. In other words, make every second count, and limit idle chatter.

To do this, assign a leader to each group. This person will be held responsible for keeping the group on task and productive. Next, ask each group to perform a SWOT analysis of your practice within a certain amount of time, say, five minutes. At our sessions, we use a timer to enforce more discipline around the task.

When the timer starts, each person should work individually, in silence, to brainstorm the first component of the SWOT analysis—the strengths of your business—for about five minutes. In the second five minutes, each individual should present their analysis of those strengths within their smaller groups while the group leader jots everyone's thoughts down.

Finally, individuals should rank the items they come up with as a group from best to worst.

Next, follow the same process for weaknesses, opportunities, and threats. Based on the results of your collective SWOT analysis, work together to set goals for the following year.

Goal Setting

Goal setting isn't as simple as slapping some thoughts on a board and calling it a day. Strong, healthy goals must have certain attributes. First, they must be achievable. For instance, if you were to say, "Our goal is to double our revenue in the next three months," that's an unrealistic goal and therefore less likely to be achieved.

Next, a strong goal must be measurable. You have to know how you'll be able to tell whether you've met your goal once it's finally met. You could tie a number to it to make it measurable, as in the above example where we specify a certain desired percentage of growth. However, assigning a number isn't required to make a goal measurable. (We'll see an example a few paragraphs from now.)

Finally, know why the goal is important to you. Ultimately, the goals you set will yield results, but you have to know what you want those results to be so that you'll know whether you achieved what you hoped to from your goals.

For instance, if you set a goal to become more profitable, you may find that to be important because you know greater profit will deliver better opportunities for everyone at the business. That's the result you should look for, then, once you've been successful in achieving that goal.

We set anywhere from three to five goals for our practice. One time, one of them was to be named the best place to work in the Capital District. Let's take that goal as an example to analyze whether it's a healthy one. First, is the goal measurable? Is it achievable? Yes, to both of those questions. (This is an example of a scenario where we don't have to tie a number to the goal to make it measurable.)

Next, you must be able to answer the question, "Why is this important?" We actually earned that award once, and for us it was important because we believed it would help us attract better talent, and it did. This means our goal was successful because it delivered the results we were hoping for.

Dr. Williams's Proven, Tested Template for Strategic Planning

If you've ever conducted a strategic planning session, you know it can be overwhelming. I spent several years massaging and fine-tuning our sessions so that they could run as seamlessly as they do today. In the process, I designed a strategic planning cheat sheet, which I'll share at the back of the book, that works beautifully for our practice. I also work from the worksheets provided in Verne Harnish's outstanding book *Scaling Up*.

You'll notice that the template consists of many parts. First, it has a place where you can map out your goals. Say, for instance, your goal was to grow your profitability by 15 percent; you'd jot that down. Then you'd ask yourself what the result of that goal would be. For instance, the 15 percent increase in profitability could offer better opportunity for growth for everyone in our practice, make our profit margins more stable, and lead to business growth, all of which would be a win-win for every party involved. Strategic planning in this way is a lot to accomplish in a day and, quite frankly, done correctly is exhausting, so once we settle on three to five goals, we break and work through each goal separately at a different time.

Typically, we take about two hours, say, on a Friday afternoon, to go through one goal. Once we come up with that goal, we go around the room and ask the group if they have any objections to the goal. We also discuss any potential obstacles to the goal. Then we come up with a strategy to overcome those obstacles.

Finally, we assign a timeline in which we can reasonably accomplish that goal. For instance, we may target a deadline of September 30 for one particular goal. To ensure we stay on track and meet that deadline, we assign a responsible party to that goal (usually someone at a manager level). This is particularly effective because tasking someone with the responsibility of monitoring the goal puts the pressure on them to stay on top of it, ensuring the goal is achieved.

We follow this process for each goal, so we limit ourselves to discussing one goal per two-hour session since the process can be pretty exhausting. During these goal-establishing sessions, we have a moderator, who serves as a drill sergeant. This person keeps us all on schedule, on task, and on topic because it's easy to digress.

As a follow-up, I touch base with the managers responsible for each goal during our regular one-on-one managers' meetings to find out how we're progressing.

The most amazing thing for me is to see the results when this process is implemented effectively. For instance, it's not unusual for me to walk the office and notice something extraordinarily different after a strategic planning session. "What's that?" I'll usually ask a manager.

"Oh, remember how we talked about getting rid of some of the confusion surrounding the front desk? Well, this chart helps us with that. Here's how it works," they'll say.

That's called effective execution in action.

Hiring a Professional

For those of you who have never held a strategic planning session, all of this may sound a little overwhelming. My advice, if this sounds like you, would be to consider hiring a facilitator who is familiar with the process and can expertly guide you through it. In almost any community, you can find skilled professionals who are familiar with running effective strategic planning sessions, and there's no shame in reaching out to them.

This year, for instance, our firm had ambitious goals to scale up on business, so we brought in a professional to lead our session. Even as someone who is experienced in taking charge of these sessions, I saw value in having this individual guide us. Ultimately, they were more than worth the investment, rounding up our leaders to create a strategic thinking team and helping us elevate our efforts to the next rung.

> # Without discussion and vigorous debate during strategic planning sessions, creativity is stifled.
>
> **Dr. Edwin Williams**

THE POWER OF MONTHLY LEADERSHIP MEETINGS

As we've established, most doctors have a disdain for meetings. I agree that ineffective meetings can be exhausting and a total waste of valuable time. Essentially, if you're doing meetings correctly, you should be leaving each one with action items to tackle and follow up on the next time you meet. However, when your day is slammed with back-to-back meetings, there's no way you can expect to have enough time to be productive. To make the most of every meeting, I jot notes in advance, skim through my notes, skim through the previous month's meeting minutes, and follow a specific agenda.

For all organizations serious about growth and gaining market share, meetings can be extremely useful for many purposes. My standard agenda and topics of conversation when meeting with managers and the chief operating officer are as follows.

Training

As I mentioned previously, I like to open my meetings with light learning for the group. I might pull a tidbit from a book I recently read or do some reinforcement learning on a topic we've touched on in the past. For instance, we studied the Ritz-Carlton's culture and read a book on it as a group, so sometimes I'll revisit a best practice of theirs. Training, I've found, gets people's minds going and is a great icebreaker.

What's Up?

Once everyone's loosened up, I go around the room asking each person to share what's up with them. I get a turn, too, at the very end and give the group a quick gist of what's up with me. These are meant to be brief exchanges of information with no detail. For example, last month, we talked about hiring another patient care coordinator, so in our latest meeting, I updated the group to share that I'd brought someone on board. My "what's up" went something like this: "Remember we were talking about hiring a new patient care coordinator? Well, I hired one today. Her name is Susan, and she's coming to us from another practice where she's worked for five years." That's it. We try to keep it short and simple.

I also like leveraging these what's-up sessions to let staff hear news directly from me versus the gossip mill. For instance, we had some issues with one of our anesthesia providers, and I had to fire someone. In our meeting, I was transparent with the group and made them aware of this, notifying them that we'd be closing the surgery center for two weeks because we no longer had an anesthesia provider. Again, this level of transparency is meant to build trust and keep rumors at bay.

KPIs

Key performance indicators are important, but you have to be cautious about how many you have. As William Bruce Cameron once said, "Not everything that can be counted counts, and not everything that counts can be counted." Essentially, you want to limit what you count and focus on the things that really matter.

Only five to seven components of your business should be included as part of your key performance indicators. For instance, in our med spa, one of the things we measure and report each month is our total revenue. Next, we look at how many units of Botox we used the previous month and also how many consultations we did. Meetings are an effective way to communicate and track KPIs and measure progress in your defined areas.

Coachings

Meetings are essential for coaching sessions. I never let my managers get by without ensuring they're spending ample time coaching. Often in managers' meetings, I'll ask them several questions to check our progress with coachings, such as "Did you talk to Rose about her strengths? What is she struggling with? What are her frustrations?"

My managers always come prepared for these questions because they're routine now. And if they haven't had a chance to touch base with a particular employee, I make sure to notate that and follow up with them in the next meeting to ensure the coaching took place. I'm purposefully persistent about this because, as I've mentioned, 70 percent of employees leave a position over frustration. When you're able to routinely tap into those frustrations and rectify what's within your control, those frustrations are less likely to remain problems for your employees.

Cultural Reinforcement

Meetings are also a great time to reinforce your culture. For instance, I'll ask managers, "Tell me specifics; what did you do last month to reinforce our culture?"

They might say, "Well, three days ago, Sarah did an incredible deed for one our patients, so in our morning huddle, I commended her for that."

When you have a few routines that you focus on regularly (such as, in this case, consistently asking how managers are helping instill our culture), this in itself becomes a part of your culture and simultaneously helps build it.

Old Business and New Business

As you'll recall, our what's-up sessions are a quick run-through of items. But in what I call our "old business/new business discussions," we expand upon those discussion points. For instance, a manager might say, "Remember that day in our what's up session, I told you we're having a problem with our equipment? Well, I wanted your opinion on it because we'll need it to build up a particular part of the practice." Again, these types of meetings (like most of my others) take about ninety minutes or so.

We've talked at length about strategic planning sessions and how to effectively lead them. Once you have a firm grasp on these, you're ready to take the next step toward growing your business. In the next chapter, we'll talk through how to do exactly that through the use of multiple profit centers.

KEY TAKEAWAYS

→ Strategic plans are an excellent way to map out where you want to see your business go.

→ Make sure you allocate enough time for your strategic planning sessions to get the most from them.

→ Be sure to engage all staff in planning sessions to ensure you're getting a well-rounded, diverse perspective from every employee in your practice.

→ A SWOT analysis and goal setting are key components of a successful strategic planning session.

→ Meetings are essential to ensuring you're executing on the goals you brainstorm in these sessions.

CHAPTER 6

MULTIPLE PROFIT CENTERS FOR THE ENTREPRENEUR PROFESSIONAL

When I was a young surgeon, I started to understand the difference between performance and leverage. I realized that even as a highly paid surgeon, my income and family revenue was limited to what I personally generated in the operating room each and every day. Then I compared that to having investments, assets, and businesses—all of which had the capability to produce revenue even while I slept. It really hit home after my accident in 2006. On Wednesday, October 25, I was foxhunting on horseback with the Old Chatham Hunt Club while trying out a new hunt horse. My horse spooked, reared with me on his back (yes, like "Hi-ho, Silver!" style), flipped over backward, and came down on me and my right leg. I ended up with a comminuted crush injury of my tibial plateau with the associated fasciotomies, external fixation, and months of rehabilitation. My orthopedic surgeon told us at the time he was most concerned about saving my leg and that most people who do save their leg never really recover from an injury of this severity to the bone and joint. I became obsessed with the rehabilitation process, determined not to have any limitations, and the following year, in 2007, I went out west to ski four times, including in the deep steep stuff. I even got my game back for skiing the bumps. (Mogul skiing is one of the biggest adrenaline rushes in life.)

I had a wheelchair fabricated for me so even at one month, once I was out of external fixation, I could do surgery from the chair. It was miserable because I was in a lot of pain between trying to operate and get comfortable. During the time I was not able to work, I distinctly remember sitting in my study one Saturday and watching a Notre Dame football game when the reality of the situation hit me head on. I realized that merely relying on yourself to generate revenue is what limits the lifetime income of professionals. For instance, with rare exception, there is a limit on how high a physician can raise fees, even if they're considered the very best. As I tried to understand business valuation during that time frame, I had an epiphany that may be common sense to most seasoned business professionals: a business that is dependent primarily on the performance of one individual has no value at all.

This concept inspired me to get to a point where doing surgery was more of a hobby or a passion—something I loved to do because I was good at it, not because I needed to do it to make sure there was food on the table. That's when I started to learn how to operate a business.

Once I learned to strategize and master the art of running that business, life became infinitely easier. My days ran on autopilot. My staff knew what was expected of them. They had policies and systems to guide them. Our culture was tangible—and what we were known for. Potential candidates were clamoring at the door, eager to be a part of our team because of it. The best part was our profits were no longer solely dependent on my being in the operating room. About 80 percent of our revenue came from my staff's ability to do their job well—only 20 percent came from my personal contributions. The day I was able to step back and see the results of those years of relentless efforts felt great.

> # I always knew I wanted to go down this road. I've made some mistakes along the way, but at a 30,000-foot view, I've won.
> **Dr. Edwin Williams**

With my business sailing smoothly, I was ready to turn my attention to the next great challenge. That's when I began exploring growth and further profitability through the introduction of profit centers.

WHAT A PROFIT CENTER IS AND RELEVANT EXAMPLES

Profit centers are essentially what they sound like; they're centers that allow you to generate passive income. Typically, these come in the form of side ventures stemming from your primary business that create smaller inflows of income. In the aesthetic space, profit centers can take on many forms. I've dabbled with many; some have done well, and others have failed miserably. At my last count, I have had at least thirty profit centers over the past many years, including my real estate ventures. But even the failures left me with priceless lessons. I'll share a few examples of those profit centers here so you have a better idea of what they can look like in the aesthetic space for a certified plastic surgeon like me.

An Overview

Medi spas that offer skin care services are an example of a profit center in the aesthetic space. Basically, these are spas through which you can administer laser treatments. Vein centers and hair transplant centers are also types of facilities that could branch into profit centers.

Alternatively, you can bring on other surgeons or practitioners or even people from fellowship programs who can work or study under you and whose services you can bill for. These offer a potential for another type of profit center.

→ **But you can also lose money, so you must be prepared to take the risk and accept the loss.**

If you wanted to take it a step further, you could launch your own skin care line. Or you may consider launching a research company that does clinical trials for drug companies.

All of these skin-related services could be side ventures you pursue from a plastic surgery practice. As you can see, it would be easy for these businesses to correlate with and tie back to one another, referring business back and forth, which makes them great options to generate maximum revenue from a single pool of patients. But you can also lose money, so you must be prepared to take the risk and accept the loss.

Real Estate

Many surgeons, me included, own their own buildings. When you have several parcels or segments of real estate that you can lease out to others, this presents an opportunity for you to generate additional income. This type of investment not only reduces your share of the payment for your space but also helps you build equity in the property over time with a smaller amount of funding required from you.

Consulting

If you're exceptional at what you do, consulting is an option that could generate a sizable side income depending on how frequently you do it and how serious you are about it. Personally, I've taken it on as a profit center. I know my time is probably better spent and more valuable in an operating room, but because I'm passionate about consulting and enjoy it, I don't mind trading time value for the joy consulting brings me. Helping other professionals or small businesspeople maximize their potential and become more successful financially makes me feel good, so I continue to consult.

Destination Practice

If you have the ability to open a practice at a distant location, say, in another state, this could be another great way to earn additional income. We have one in St. Thomas that's been fairly successful. However, managing a destination practice requires strong talent and staff that can effectively and faithfully manage the practice so that you're able to make profit from it without having to split your time between managing it and running your other locations.

BENEFITS OF PROFIT CENTERS

Why consider having profit centers if you're already running a practice? By now, the answer's probably obvious. Profit centers help accelerate your wealth acquisition over time. Not only do they enable you to make money, but they also empower you to build equity.

The other benefit profit centers carry is that they give you something to sell. For instance, through the use of profit centers, I now have both real estate and a surgery center I can one day list for sale, which also makes way for wealth accumulation.

These are certainly the upsides of profit centers, but here's a word of caution: running a profit center isn't everyone's cup of tea, and you can lose tons of money in it if you don't take it seriously, lack business skills, or don't know what you're doing. To determine whether pursuing a profit center is the right move for you, you should consider several questions.

QUESTIONS TO ASK BEFORE INVESTING IN PROFIT CENTERS

As entrepreneurs, we have a tendency to think the grass is most definitely greener on the other side. We look at one venture and then another, and our minds start whirring with wonder: "Will I make more money here? Or is it actually more lucrative over there?" In reality, the best thing to do is assess the situation and ask yourself several questions before taking the plunge into profit centers.

First, ask yourself why you're interested in profit centers. Why are you looking to venture beyond being a doctor or a "technician," as I like to call it? Is it because you're seeking diversification? Are you looking to make money? Are you after a challenge? Are you looking for greater exposure to cross-sell other services? If you've answered yes to these questions, it's time to probe deeper into others to find out whether you're really ready to take the leap.

Is Your Practice in Order?

I can't tell you how many times I've looked at colleagues' profit-and-loss statements and balance sheets only to realize their practices are a complete mess. Frequently, they're overstaffed, their books are a nightmare, they haven't created a separate legal entity for their business, and they have no idea of the fair market value of their time and business. Most surprisingly, many of them don't even know whether they're truly even profitable after taking into consideration the fair market value of their doctors' time.

You can't and shouldn't attempt other ventures if your existing one is in a state of disarray. Getting your practice in order and knowing it inside out is essential before you go down the path toward pursuing other ventures. I always recommend *The E-Myth Revisited*, by Michael Gerber, for those looking to pursue entrepreneurship. Many people who take my advice and read it agree that it's one of the best books out there and creates a clear business perspective. It's also a great knowledge source regarding the topic of profit centers.

Are You Making Time to Work on Your Business?

As we know, spending time on your business is just as important for physicians as spending time *in* it is.

When considering profit centers, evaluate whether you'll have enough time to devote to them, just like you do for your business. Like any other asset or relationship, profit centers will require it, so if you're already stretched thin or only able to contribute the bare minimum hours, you should probably reconsider.

Is the Model Profitable?

Before you commit to invest in profit centers, make sure they'll be an investment worth your dollars and time. Will the center be profitable? What's the potential profit margin? When you take your gross and subtract your expenses, you should have at least 10 percent left over for the venture to be considered worthwhile. If you have 20 percent remaining after everything's said and done, you've found a winner.

Jack Welsh has been quoted as saying that one question you should constantly ask yourself about your businesses is this: If I weren't in my current business, would I get into it again? If the answer is no, you should probably consider selling or liquidating because some business models truly prove to be nothing more than an uphill battle, stealing valuable energy and time better spent elsewhere. It is imperative to have the intestinal fortitude to exit a business rather than hold onto something for posterity or a variety of other dysfunctional reasons.

> → Truth be told, some businesses are just crappy by nature.

Truth be told, some businesses are just crappy by nature. Our surgery center, for example, constantly struggles to break even each year. So why do I stay in it? Because it has other intangible benefits. I have the luxury of being able to do surgery in my own facility with my own staff in a private and efficient setting. So even if the center only breaks even, these benefits are enough to make me a happy guy.

Can You Systemize It?

Earlier we discussed the importance of systems and policies, so asking yourself whether your profit centers can be systemized is an essential question to ponder. Can you make it into a turnkey operation? Can you scale it up? Can you create policies around its operation? Or are you trading dollars for time? If the answer to that last question is yes, the venture probably isn't worth the sacrifice.

What Are Your Barriers to Entry?

Observe the skin care landscape, and you'll notice huge brands dominate the industry. When I first started, I didn't realize or consider that. I simply looked at the money potential and figured we'd be profitable. However, scoping out your barriers to entry is critical because it's hard to penetrate a market where competition is heavy.

However, if you happen to be in an industry or space with low barriers to entry, don't get too excited. Sooner or later, competition is sure to crop up. To remain a leader and stay ahead of the curve, you must maintain strong knowledge of the market.

There's a woman in our town who owns a 40,000-square-foot skin care facility. She's been in day spa magazines and is pretty well known around town. Would I ever dare to compete with her? Probably not.

The other side of that equation to consider is whether you have unique advantages you could boast over the competition. Is there an element or ability that would distinguish you from competitors and lower your barriers to entry? If so, these could heighten your chances of success. If not, you're likely better off walking away.

In 2006, we opened a medi spa in Saratoga Springs, about twenty miles from our current practice. We didn't understand the market. Instead, we figured that because we were successful in our current model, we could achieve the same success in Saratoga.

That was a big mistake. The area was provincial, and people viewed us as outsiders. A quarter of a million dollars in, we pulled the plug and closed down the business—all because we failed to scope out the market landscape. It's a risk we took due to lack of knowledge, which is one of the key reasons businesses fail.

OTHER CONSIDERATIONS

As you're looking into profit centers, one thing to understand is that nothing beats the scalpel per unit of time. I say that because often, when we're considering these side ventures, we have a tendency to wonder if we can make as much, or more, on skin care products than we can in an operating room. The reality is we can't. Side ventures such as profit centers aren't meant to be your primary revenue-generating resource—they're simply meant to supplement what you're already making.

Another important component to think about when you're deciding whether a profit center is right for you is whether you'll enjoy it. As they say, you are what you do, not what you say. If you really appreciate the business side of things, adding profit centers is probably a good direction to travel toward.

For me, being successful in business, growing it, and making more money feels like a game. I enjoy it, and I enjoy winning. If you don't, the emotional and financial burden of it all can be enough to burn you out, in which case you're better off sticking to familiar territory in the operating room.

Also, know whether you're risk averse. If you're not a prudent risk-taker, you'll have no business. If you're a reckless risk-taker, you'll lose money hand over fist.

There's no shortcut to reward—if you want to see the rewards, you must take the risk and work at it.

Dr. Edwin Williams

If you're thinking about investing in profit centers, another aspect of business you should enjoy is meeting with consultants, accountants, and other talents to make sure things are running smoothly. Personally, I'm all about that because to me, business is about human behavior, which is something that's always held my interest. I love understanding why people purchase things, and I love learning how I can level up my practice and ventures by observing professionals.

Leadership, team building, and management should also be interests because you'll be engaging in these heavily as you expand and grow your businesses. Books such as *Good to Great*, by Jim Collins, and *Winning*, by Jack Welch, have great information on these topics.

Bigger Isn't Better

The costliest expense for nearly any business is staff. Often, entrepreneurs tend to think that having more employees is better—you're able to serve more customers, see more people, and rake in more money. But if you're not great at managing, building, and holding your team accountable, the costs you'll see as a result of these deficiencies may eat you alive. A large staff can weigh more heavily on your budget—with more payroll, more people making errors—if you don't effectively manage it. That's also where leadership skills come into play. Great leaders have the ability to influence, meaning less physical effort and emotional stress on your end to single-handedly "manage" staff.

REASONS TO MOVE FORWARD

If you feel pretty positive about your answers to the previous questions and are more confident than ever that profit centers align well with your goals, you're ready for the final round of vetting to see whether you have the green light to move forward.

You're Passionate about It Despite the Pitfalls

We had a skin care professional who was one of my best sources of referrals in town for my skin care company. To say thank you for sending so much business my way, I gifted her a minority interest in our skin care company—without a dime of investment from her.

Although the business wasn't losing money, it wasn't making money either. So when I had an opportunity to sell, I did. The referrer got a payout, even though she hadn't put forth a penny. However, she grew upset because she felt that we should have kept the business a bit longer. For the last twenty years, she hasn't sent me a single patient. God knows what that has cost me over the past twenty-five years.

The moral of the story? You may stumble into several unintended consequences from your profit centers, perhaps things you never anticipated or expected. But you should feel passionate enough about the venture to still pursue it. If the passion isn't there, the effort won't be either.

It's Supportive of Your Current Business

Your profit center should, ideally, complement your core business. As a facial plastic surgeon, it makes sense for me to have profit centers related to skin care because one can feed off the other without stretching too much of me and my time in a different direction. If your centers don't support your core business, I'd recommend reevaluating—you don't want to enter into something that steals time from your core business.

Back in 1994 I started a skin care company. It was successful, but I realized it was a distraction that was robbing me of my time, so I ended up selling it after just two years. As my father once said, "Time isn't money; time is life." We opened a vein center many years ago only to close it after two years of headaches and very limited profit. God knows what this distraction cost me in opportunity cost by taking my valuable time away from more financially productive activities.

You're Ready to Take the Risk

Every small business owner has the worst job—because ultimately, you're on the hook with the bank, personally guaranteeing the success or failure of your business. The bank won't assume that risk.

For instance, when our surgery center was losing money, guess who was on the line to move money out of their personal bank account? Me. I had to cover payroll, rent, and overhead costs. Risk is an inherent part of business—there's never any guarantee that you'll make money.

> # The only regrets I have in life are the things I didn't do.
> ## Dr. Edwin Williams

The only reason to start a business/profit center, or grow one, is for equity and/or wealth accumulation or to have something in hand to sell at the end.

You're Looking to Diversify

If you're ready to branch out into something new because you want growth or a new challenge, you're probably ready to invest in profit centers. As I mentioned, only 20 percent of my income is generated from me performing surgeries. I have my hands in so many different profit centers that I'm not worried if something happens to me because I know my family wouldn't suffer—that's the power of diversification.

MUSTS FOR PROFIT CENTERS

Profit centers should have a few characteristics; these generally augment their chances of success and make them worth your time and money. Here are the ones I most commonly seek—and the ones I suggest you look for too.

Must Stand Alone

All profit centers must stand alone as a profitable business model. To determine whether a venture you're considering has the capability to stand alone, it's imperative you keep accurate cost accounting.

That means knowing the rent, utilities, general liability, staff, and maintenance costs. If the center is making money after you account for all expenses, it's profitable and can stand alone, meaning it can sufficiently sustain itself.

If you're not sure how to tackle cost accounting or numbers simply aren't your forte, that's fine, but I'd highly recommend you secure the help of an accountant—numbers are important.

Must Deliver Value

I remember one time when we made a few equipment purchases that didn't make good sense because they didn't deliver value to us or our clients. Value should be a critical focus of your business—in fact, anything you put money toward in your profit center must be truly efficacious.

In our business, people tend to place high importance on FDA-approved products, but what they don't understand is that the FDA label is just for safety. Many products that are FDA approved don't work well or demonstrate quality—that's where, in my opinion, they fall short. If a patient's going to spend thousands of dollars on our treatments, I want to ensure we're delivering true value because that's their satisfaction and my reputation on the line.

Must Pay for Itself

When you factor in cost accounting, any technology or equipment you put your money behind should pay for itself in two years. Technology in particular can be a major risk and setback because it has the potential to change rapidly from one day to the next. One minute something could be in vogue, and the next, it could become totally dated. Again, cost accounting will be able to help you calculate which risks can repay their own costs within two years and which ones can't.

LESSONS TO LEARN

My businesses, as you can tell, haven't always been smooth sailing. I've learned plenty on my journey of exploring profit centers. I've taken notes after failures and successes, so I am able to adapt for the future. I can't think of a single time when I've walked away from a situation without a moral or lesson learned. Below, I share the most notable ones. Consider them words of wisdom that I hope you don't have the misfortune of having to unveil all on your own.

Hire a Health-Care Attorney

I would advise any health-care professional out there to first and foremost hire an attorney to guide you in manners of legality. This might seem to be an overly cautious step, but I can assure you that one misstep may cost you both your reputation and career, so as they say, better safe than sorry.

I've seen colleagues and mentees engage in all sorts of activities that are considered either misconduct or plain out illegal simply because they didn't know better.

For example, colleagues of mine have paid their nurses a certain percentage from their business. This is called fee splitting or revenue sharing with a nonphysician, which is considered misconduct.

Unfortunately, malpractice insurance doesn't cover lawsuits for medical misconduct, which can cost you heavily. A colleague of mine was once investigated for it and spent over $100,000 in legal defense.

An experienced health-care attorney can help you easily sidestep these unnecessary risks because they will know the laws within your industry and practice. The key is hiring someone who is intimately familiar with your field and knows the regulations surrounding it. One of my friends once drafted the services of an attorney, but because they weren't specialized in health care, they couldn't offer prudent advice, and my friend ended up unknowingly engaging in fee splitting. Of course, these circumstances aren't a problem until they're a problem, but hiring the right attorney can help prevent them from ever becoming one. Just remember, all it takes is one disgruntled employee to unleash a nightmare on your business.

Profit Center Red Flags

Now that we've talked about all the questions you should ask yourself and what you should look for in a profit center, I want to turn your attention to red flags you should beware of when you're managing profit centers. One of the major ones is to ensure you're not overleveraging yourself. If the bills are getting tight and it's becoming difficult to make ends meet, something's not right, and you should stop before matters get worse. I can tell you from personal experience that moving thousands of dollars from one account to the other to cover bills is never a good feeling—even when you have the money, it hurts.

If you don't have the money, it's even worse because that could mean that you've possibly put your entire savings, not to mention credit, at stake. That's why living well within your means and only using what you know you have is crucial.

Not having any money set aside for a rainy day is another major red flag. That means you're expecting to tide yourself over from one month to the next on pure luck, which is asking for trouble. To avoid a terrible situation where one dry month causes your business to lag—or worse, collapse—apply for lines of credit well in advance, before you even need them.

When we were hitting rock bottom financially with our surgery center, we were able to stay afloat thanks to a line of credit I tapped into to cover payroll. With a quick phone call, that money was available to me—all because I'd prepared in advance.

We've talked about alternative streams of income that can supplement your earnings from your primary practice. But there's another integral topic that goes hand in hand with your efforts as you embark on these journeys of pursuing multiple businesses and profits centers: how to avoid burnout and maintain a healthy work–life balance. That's what we'll tackle in the next chapter.

KEY TAKEAWAYS

→ Profit centers are great as additional income and revenue streams that supplement your primary income.

→ Ideally, profit centers should complement your primary practice—not pull attention away from it.

→ Strong profit centers must stand alone, deliver value, and pay for themselves.

→ To be successful as a profit center and business, make sure you're not overleveraging yourself financially and that you have enough money set aside for a rainy day through tools such as personal funds and lines of credit.

CHAPTER 7

LIFE BALANCE FOR THE PHYSICIAN ENTREPRENEUR AND HOW TO AVOID BURNOUT

A Mormon fellow of mine once said, "No success at work justifies failure at home." I couldn't agree more. As a father of four, I can't tell you how many times I've seen colleagues suffer the pain of seeing their children through rehab—all because they spent precious time focusing on their profession instead of raising their kids.

Early on in my career, I knew I didn't want to be *that* parent—the workaholic—so that's what I focused on *not being*. My work schedule revolved around my children's practices and performances. Colleagues would approach me, bewildered. "I can't believe you rework your entire schedule around your family and kids," they'd say.

Jokingly, I'd tell reply, "It's cheaper than spending a quarter of a million bucks on rehab, which by the way, doesn't always work the first time."

Personally, I believe the stakes are too high to *not* center your work around family. Divorce, neglected children, and broken relationships are too high a price to pay. To me, as my Mormon friend stated, no amount of success was worth the failure. But when you're a physician, learning how to strike the right balance can prove tricky. However, with the right strategy and mind-set, it's more than doable.

→ Early on in my career, I knew I didn't want to be *that* parent—the workaholic—so that's what I focused on *not being.*

INVESTING TIME AT WORK

We think, mistakenly, that success is the result of the amount of time we put in at work, instead of the quality of time we put in.

—Arianna Huffington, founder of the *Huffington Post*

When I attended fellowship training, my mentor was a man named Dr. T. This man had a world-class practice, a world-class reputation, and a world-class record of being out the door at five o'clock on the nose. He was extremely efficient, and he taught me that this level of efficiency was not only possible but necessary—because leaving late takes its toll on your family.

A neighbor of mine was a CEO of a publicly traded company that employed over a thousand people. He worked until six or seven each night, most nights. But when he was home, he stowed away the laptop and shut off his cell phone so he could spend quality time with his family. It's possible to be extremely effective without investing too many man-hours. Understanding and practicing that balance and discipline is crucial—not only with yourself but with your staff too.

At work, for example, I value my staff for how hard and effectively they work, not for how long they spend at the office. As I once said to a graduate student body during a commencement speech at the University of Illinois, "You can do it all. You just can't do it all at once." And you shouldn't try to either.

In medicine, where it can feel like you're running an endless marathon, this is particularly essential to remember. When you try too hard to do too much altogether, it's easy to find yourself repetitively cycling through exhaustion and recovery, which can ultimately lead to burnout.

THE SIGNS AND SYMPTOMS OF BURNOUT

The term *burnout* was first used in 1974 by Herbert Freudenberger, the author of the book *Burnout*. Since then it's become common vocabulary in the US—particularly in the medical profession.

A family friend near and dear to me used to practice medicine and was married to an ophthalmologist. One day, out of the blue, she announced she was quitting her profession. Her revelation both shocked and saddened me. I know she, like the rest of us, had invested time and energy behind pursuing her degree. For her to toss it away, I sensed, must have been a huge move and a decision she hadn't taken lightly. When I approached her to see what had influenced her move, her response was swift. "I'm burned out," she said. "I can't do it anymore." Unfortunately, hers is a story all too common in our profession. By the way she was thirty-eight years old when she made this decision. She was an incredible doctor.

> # Recognizing burnout— and most importantly, preventing it—are essential to your success and your continued appreciation of your profession.
> **Dr. Edwin Williams**

If you suspect you're feeling fatigued or bogged down, here are three big signs and symptoms indicating that you could be suffering burnout.

Emotional Exhaustion

When you feel both physically and emotionally drained, that's a major indication that something's not quite right. Emotionally, you may feel disinterested or lacking excitement to wake up and kick-start your day. You may no longer look forward to the operating room or seeing patients. This isn't the same as having a general dislike of your career, which some physicians experience from the onset of their professions. It's more of a transformation. One day you wake up passionate about your career, and the next you jolt awake in the middle of the night, dreading what you do. Physically, you may feel sluggish, lazy, down, and despondent.

Depersonalization

Everyone has the displeasure of facing unreasonable patients every now and again—the ones who are unbearable, dramatic, or just plain out irritating. Every profession sees them, the medical profession being no exception. You bite your tongue to hold back a sarcastic remark or imagine pulling your hair out strand by strand in frustration. That's normal. However, when you're feeling burned out, this once-in-a-rare-occasion irritation can feel like a constant presence in your life. You easily become cynical, callous, and dismissive of nearly everyone and their feelings, regardless of who they are. Often, these sentiments trickle on over toward your staff as well.

Physicians suffering burnout have often come to me and said, "I can't stand my patients anymore." They start to become less caring, empathetic, and compassionate toward them. This is a red flag.

Reduced Sense of Accomplishment

Another sign of burnout is a reduced sense of accomplishment. When I was in this phase at one point in my career, I would spend six to eight hours in the operating room performing procedure after procedure. But when the gloves came off and the lights shut down, I didn't feel the usual sense of fulfillment. For physicians it's easy to become disengaged and grow disinterested in what we do and stick it out in this phase for a while.

BURNOUT AMONG PHYSICIANS

Certain studies prove that at any one time, 30–70 percent of physicians describe themselves as feeling burned out.[1] The way I see it, burnout among physicians is a somewhat uphill battle for several reasons.

Job Stress

Being in medicine is a stressful job, no matter how you look at it. You're often caught running from one patient to the next, and sometimes you may need to do the physically impossible, like be in two places at once. The worst part is that despite your best efforts, you don't always have control over outcomes. For instance, during face-lift surgery, I have at least one patient every now and again who encounters complications. This kind of responsibility over human lives is mentally and physically draining.

Difficulty Separating Work from Life

Doctors commonly have a challenging time separating work from life—once they lock up for the day and head home, they're still not able to gain distance from work. Many of them are on call with their cell phones at the ready, constantly worrying, constantly thinking about their patients. They develop a Pavlovian response to the phone, which affects their personal lives.

The other element that makes matters worse is that several physicians run their own practices, which comes with its own set of drawbacks. For instance, take my surgery center, a brutal business where it's near impossible to break even. I've lost more sleep over

---

1   Dan Lee, Ben McIntire, and Edwin Williams, "Career Satisfaction, Commitment and Burnout among Facial Plastic Surgeons" (presented at Resident Research Day, June 14, 2019).

it than any other business platform I have. Even after I leave the practice to go home, it's difficult to leave those worries behind in the operating room.

Patients Relying Heavily on You

As a physician, you're constantly looked upon to meet the needs of patients. Most will come to you expecting your complete time, attention, and focus. Doctors who treat ill patients, for instance, are required to tend to, reassure, and placate them, diminishing any fears and doubts. This level of responsibility is both physically and emotionally draining, not to mention a big stressor.

Keeping Up with Time

When you work a nine-to-five, you're up against deadlines, which is most people's main struggle. However, as a physician, your greatest challenge is keeping to the clock—minute by minute—from one patient to the next. A five-minute delay with the first patient could throw you off by two hours by the end of the day, which not only frustrates people but is also mentally and physically exhausting for you.

When I'm in the operating room, I'm habitually watching the clock. The worst part is even if I am falling behind, there's no rushing through my work. I'm forced to take my time with each patient, giving them the care they deserve—there's no magical solution to creating more time. At the end of the day, however, that lack of control is stressful.

A High-Investment Profession

Physicians are considered extremely invested in their occupations. They spend years training and making financial and personal sacrifices along the way. In most other careers, once you go through schooling and enter your profession, you have the ability to pull the plug on your career at any time, switching gears and jumping into a different profession if you want. Skills gleaned in one career path can easily be carried over to another profession. But in the medical profession, that's not the case. You spend several years becoming highly specialized in one thing and one thing only, to the point that those specialized skills cannot be of use anywhere else. Your career is yours for life—unless you decide to go back to school or start from ground zero with meager pay in an entry-level position. Being that invested in a career is stressful, making you more susceptible to burnout. Most feel chained to their profession with no easy exit, so they continue to work until they simply don't have it in them to continue any longer.

Leadership

Physicians don't receive formalized training in leadership, which can hinder the effectiveness and longevity of their business. Running a business means knowing how to be a leader—and to do that you should enroll in leadership training. However, most doctors don't bother learning these skills, which only adds to the burden of managing a practice.

Financial and Patient Frustrations

The Affordable Care Act has been a source of exasperation for many doctors across the nation, which is why more are exiting the profession today than ever before. The financial considerations in value delivery coupled with frustrations related to coding, preapprovals, and denials of procedures already performed all serve as additional stressors.

I once did a rhinoplasty on a physician who had preapproval for the procedure from his insurance company. Just to be safe, I got opinions from two insurance claims agents to ensure the claims wouldn't fall through and I'd get paid on time. I performed the surgery only to have the insurance company come back eight months later and deny the claim. Now I'm stuck fighting appeals.

Other frustrations include displeased and dissatisfied patients. Also, the heightened sensitivity around compliance doesn't help, with new policies frequently being introduced into the practice of medicine.

Paperwork and the loss of autonomy are the cherry on top. A frustrated urologist friend of mine called me recently. "Ed, I have to get out of this," he said. "I see maybe twenty patients and am here until six or seven o'clock every night with all this documentation and compliance crap. I can't seem to break above water."

As they say, the struggle is real.

Malpractice

Most doctors care deeply about their patients, but no matter how great a job you do, you can't avoid the occasional malpractice suit. Typically these take about two to three years before they even see the light of a courthouse, and they can be extremely taxing.

Once, I got sued and spent a month in court. After dozens of days fretting and several endless sleepless nights, the only minutes that mattered were the few it took to announce the final verdict—the vote was unanimous: I won. Case over. However, that month sucked the life out of me. I remember finishing that court case and thinking, "If I had enough money right now, I'd quit."

Boredom

When you do the same thing day in and day out, it's easy to grow restless and demotivated. In the surgical practice, it's a little more difficult for boredom to set in because every day brings something new. However, I wouldn't exactly consider doing twelve colonoscopies a day riveting work, so I could see something like that quickly growing tedious for me.

Routine, mundane tasks or the lack of challenges can hinder you intellectually and make your work seem monotonous and meaningless. Plus, after you spend several years consistently studying, growing your knowledge base, sharpening your mind, learning new skills, and taking tough exams only to suddenly emerge from the rabbit hole into a career where your day to day doesn't vary much, it can be mind numbing.

The Gap Concept

There's an organization called Strategic Coach that has introduced the gap concept. Personally, I think this concept is partly responsible for burnout. The "gap" in the gap concept refers to the chasm between the things you've accomplished in your life or career and the things you believe you *should* have accomplished. Many times, entrepreneurs or high-performing achievers focus on such gaps and then constantly struggle to bridge them, accelerating fatigue and stress.

WHAT TO DO TO AVOID BURNOUT

Now that we know what causes burnout, let's talk about what you can do to avoid it so you can achieve a better work–life balance and a career that brings you fulfillment and happiness.

For physicians, creating a work–life balance requires an intentional effort because the stakes are huge. Without this balance you're placing your happiness, fulfillment, marriage, and relationships on the line. You can always make more money, but no one has the coveted ability to prolong life for others or themselves.

Let's say the average person's life expectancy is around eighty. That's about forty-two million minutes—none of which I, or you, should be willing to waste. That time is best allocated for people we love and care about: family, friends, neighbors, colleagues. Some intentional steps on your part will ensure most of that time is invested in people instead of at work.

Be Aware

Without acknowledging that a healthy work–life balance is important, you'll never be able to make it a priority, let alone a possibility, in your life. As I mentioned, the stakes are too high to overlook the importance of such discipline.

Each morning, I get up at least forty-five minutes to an hour before I have to get to work. I brew my coffee and do what some might consider meditation or prayer.

Next, I intentionally go through the list of things I'm grateful for. I think about every single one of my family members, our health, and the fact that I have ambition and material possessions. Instead of focusing on the gaps in my life, I focus on the fillers that keep me whole. Do that on a regular basis, and you'll realize there's a lot to be thankful for. If you're lacking things to

> → If you're lacking things to count among your greatest blessings, just watch the news—I promise you'll whip out a list of things you're grateful for in no time.

count among your greatest blessings, just watch the news—I promise you'll whip out a list of things you're grateful for in no time.

Make a List of Your Priorities

One thing you should always make time for is organizing your priorities. I always say priorities are what you do, not what you say. Is your family really a priority? Or do you just say they are because that's what you think or would like to believe? Do you show that they're your priority? Or do you prioritize everything before them? I suggest creating a list of what's most important to you and then placing it somewhere you can easily reference or see it every day. This way you're always clear on what's most important.

Learn to Delegate and Say No

Around 2005 I started putting in way too many hours at work. Part of it had to do with the pressure of supporting a young family, but I was also early in my career and driven, so I was eager to work. Sometime the next year, I had a terrible riding accident where a horse came down on my leg and crushed it. I was in the hospital for a week and a half. Naturally, in this state, I couldn't be everywhere, so I started to push things off my slate and to say no. I learned that, from a leadership standpoint, if someone could do something 80 percent as well as I could, I wasn't willing to trade my time for money. I would rather delegate the task.

With this realization, I started combing through my daily, weekly, and monthly routines to see what was important to me and what wasn't.

For example, the American Cancer Society is a wonderful organization, and at the time I was on its board. However, I didn't have many cancer patients and I didn't feel I was contributing much, so I resigned.

Next, my kids' school invited me to be on its school board. I interviewed several people on the board to find out whether participating would be a worthy contribution of my time. A friend of mine who was a board member told me, "Ed, look, let me put it this way. We're more of a consultative board. The chairman really makes all the decisions."

Okay, I thought to myself, this isn't something I'm really interested in because it's not like I'll have a chance to make a true impact. Similar to what I was forced to do, you too should clean off your slate of engagements every now and again.

One thing to know, however, is that life changes. So what was once considered important to you may no longer be and vice versa. Just because something didn't pique your interest yesterday doesn't mean it won't ever again. That's why routinely reevaluating your engagements to ensure that they're a good use of your time and that they bring you a sense of fulfillment is essential.

Set Goals

Steve Siebold, a well-known author, launched a program called Mental Toughness. In it, you're encouraged to complete an exercise where you craft your five-year vision statement as though you're writing a letter to a friend. You're asked to identify seven or eight categories that are really important to you personally—it's almost like doing a strategic planning session for your personal life. In completing that exercise, I identified these eight categories of interest for myself.

Faith

When the kids were younger, I remember how challenging it was to participate in church activities. One day in particular, my wife and I had managed to trudge our van through town in the middle of a terrible snowstorm with the kids in tow. Snowflakes were flying sideways in an endless sheet when we rumbled into the church parking lot, so we pulled in close to the church door to let the kids out from the back. When we turned around, they were all sitting with their shoes spread everywhere, jackets tossed about and socks flung off. My wife and I looked at each other. "Dunkin' Donuts?" I said.

Now that they're older, we have more opportunities to embrace our faith by becoming involved in church activities and events we weren't able to when the kids were younger. This proves my earlier statement about how priorities and the things you make time for can shift over time.

Family

My wife loves to watch movies, but I'm not much of a movie person. However, because I know she enjoys it, I make sure that at least once or twice a month, we watch one together. We also make time for date night on Fridays, just the two of us, which I think is important. With small children, it's easy to go days without completing a single thought to each other because of interruptions and distractions all around you, but conversation is integral to building a strong relationship with your spouse. I have friends who are empty nesters and spent so much time focusing on their children that when those kids went off to college, they could no longer relate to each other. They lost their connection because they forgot to make time to nurture and rekindle their relationship.

Friends

Each month, I try to do something meaningful with my friends. This is an area I typically fall short in and need to improve on.

My daughter once said to me, "Dad, you know what? You don't have nearly as many friends as Mom does."

"You're right," I told her. "Between work and you guys, there's not much left for anyone else."

And it's true. Because I know this is a shortcoming of mine, I've set goals, like I normally do at the beginning of the year, to see how well I'm tracking in spending time with my friends. It's certainly more challenging to make time for more people when you have kids, but I know once we're empty nesters, this is one of those priorities that will inch higher up in my life.

Finances

Being meticulous with my finances is another priority high on my list. When I work our household finances, not only do I focus on how I think our savings account should be tracking but also what I believe my net worth should be. To me, this is all important because I've seen that discipline in this area is what brings freedom. I've watched several of my friends work for paychecks and chase the dollar, but by the time they reach their fifties or sixties, nothing's changed. They're still chasing. They're not free. Discipline in this area, however, has helped me cancel my disability and life insurance. I no longer need them. This sort of freedom and peace of mind comes with being very intentional about where you spend your time and how you balance your life so that you're free—because finances are one of the major known sources of stress among people. In fact, many marriages fail due to finances alone.

Business/Personal Development

As you know by now, I love learning and building knowledge. I'm extremely intentional about how many books I read each year. I'm intentional about doing strategic planning sessions for our practices. For years I was fanatical about how many professional development meetings I attended in my specialty because I wanted to be ahead of the pack. Even today, self-learning and development continue to be a priority for me.

Fitness

It's not easy to carve time out for a fitness regime when you've got a demanding career in one corner and a family in the other. Now that my kids are a little older, however, I'm better able to focus on my health and well-being. You could say I'm obsessed with it. In fact, I'm six pounds off my high school weight. Although I'm not going to beat myself up over those last few pounds, my point is that unless you're intentional about what you want to achieve, you'll fall short. That's why goal setting and writing down your priorities is an important part of the process.

Recreation/Fun

Recreation is one of those categories that changes from year to year for me. Once upon a time, I was very involved with foxhunting and horses. Now I have so many days each year I'd prefer to hit the ski slopes and so many days I'd prefer to fly—those are my current fixations. Focusing on several interests besides your career is important for everyone; otherwise, life can grow dull and boring very fast.

Social and Cultural

My wife and I feel that it's important for us to be able to give to others financially. I'd rather drive an eight-year-old car with tons of miles and donate to those in need than waste dollars on a newer model I know I can do without. My wife and I, for instance, set up a family scholarship at Siena College several years ago that now funds education for several students. Every year, we meet the kids who benefit from this foundation, and it humbles us to see the impact it has on their lives. We also donate through many other organizations. There's a reason why people such as Bill Gates, Warren Buffett, and many others are deliberate about where they put their money—because there's no better feeling than when you give.

What to Do Once You've Set Your Goals

Again, once you're through with goal setting, write a letter to a friend where you go through the categories most important to you. It might sound cheesy, but I can tell you from personal experience that it works. One time, I retrieved my goals for 2005 and compared them to the ones I established in 2010; I got goose bumps looking at all the things I'd actually accomplished.

TYING IT UP

A work–life balance is essential for professionals traveling the path of entrepreneurship. No physician ever on their deathbed said, "Darn, if only I'd performed just one more face-lift." The regrets we harbor have to do with lost family vacations or missed baseball games.

True happiness, as we know, doesn't come from money. It comes from a combination of success and fulfillment.

Dr. Edwin Williams

Life is too short to go through years of feeling absolutely miserable in your career because ultimately, no career is worth that level of self-sacrifice. Many people I know who are high achievers attain significant financial success. They climb the proverbial mountain, get where they want to be, and then look over the edge only to see a big, gaping hole staring back at them. They have no spouse, no family, and no friends by their side. The relationships they do have grow empty and hollow—all because they sacrificed them for work.

KEY TAKEAWAYS

➜ The stakes are high if you don't create a work–life balance; you may be risking your family, happiness, and mental health.

➜ Recognize the signs and symptoms of burnout so you can prevent too much damage.

➜ Make time for your personal life so your professional one doesn't take over.

➜ Prioritize the categories of your life most important to you; then set goals to ensure those categories always remain at the top of the list for you.

➜ The fulfillment you gain from family and friends is far weightier than any you can gain from financial achievements.

CHAPTER 8

SUCCESSION PLANNING AND EXIT

About ten years into my practice, an anesthesiologist I trained with in Syracuse brought his daughter in for a rhinoplasty. Postsurgery, I came out to speak with him, and he said, "Hey, Ed. You did it!"

"Huh? Did what?" I said, confused.

"I mean, you did this," he said. "When you were an intern, you were so excited about how you'd build this center one day. And you've actually done it. I'm in awe."

He was right, I thought. I had a faint recollection of once aspiring to own my own center. This realization amazed me just as much as my achievement of my goals had amazed him because it made me appreciate that I must have had some sort of plan in mind from the start—which is the key to a successful business.

But just planning how you'll get *into* business isn't enough. You must also give thought to how you'd like to exit your business once the timing's right. This is called succession or exit planning—and as an entrepreneur, it's an absolutely critical step you'll need to take.

Enter business with an exit in mind. That's the only way to do it.

Dr. Edwin Williams

In 2003 I was in London making a presentation at a meeting. Once my presentation ended, one of my esteemed elderly colleagues turned to me and said, "Ed, I'm working like crazy and running around everywhere. I'm exhausted. I haven't even given retirement a thought."

I was shocked at how much this colleague was working and juggling at his age. He had kids in college, hefty monthly bills, and an endless work schedule so he could bring home enough dough to make ends meet. I remember looking at him and thinking, *My God. With all he's got going on, this man is going to work himself to death.*

I'd love to tell you he wasn't the norm and that many doctors don't stumble into similar predicaments, but that's not true. I can't tell you how many times I've attended national meetings and met physicians closing in on their fifties and sixties who have no exit or succession plan to gracefully step out of their practices.

They'll come to me, saying, "Hey, Ed. Do you mind if I pay you a visit sometime? I'm thinking about retirement, and I know you have worked this whole thing out, but I really haven't given it much thought."

For professionals who are considered to belong to an esteemed profession and are generally considered highly intelligent, why is exit planning such a common problem? It's actually due to several reasons.

REASONS PHYSICIANS FAIL AT SUCCESSION PLANNING

One of my colleagues and I did a formal study in which we sent a survey to a population of 1,400 plastic surgeons and asked them a series of questions.[2] We presented our findings at the American Academy of Facial Plastic and Reconstructive Surgery annual fall meeting in 2018. Of the 1,400 surgeons, we received responses from 193, and we found that 16 percent of them felt they were doing a decent job running their business and leveraging their time. About 58 percent were concerned they were losing their patients to the competition. Yet 98 percent of them felt they didn't have a well-thought-out exit or succession plan. Why not? These were the most common reasons.

Procrastination Due to Competing Priorities

We all procrastinate, but physicians get so busy responding to the market that they end up working the majority of the time with their heads buried in the sand. Because they're required to remain laser focused on day-to-day patients, stay on time for appointments, and make sure everything is running smoothly, they push thoughts of the distant future—such as succession planning—to the wayside.

Ignorance Due to Lack of Knowledge

The other reason for their inaction is one we've previously touched on—lack of knowledge. Many physicians are so busy learning, by trial and error, how to run a successful practice for today that they don't realize they should be planning for tomorrow too.

---

2   Chelsea Obourn, MD, and Edwin Williams, MD, presented at the American Academy of Facial Plastic and Reconstructive Surgery annual fall meeting, Dallas, October 2018, submitted for publication.

However, spinning your wheels and paying your dues today won't do you any good if you're not preparing for the future. I call this lack of planning the entrepreneur's Achilles' heel because it single-handedly can set people up for failure come retirement time.

> → However, spinning your wheels and paying your dues today won't do you any good if you're not preparing for the future.

Also, many physician entrepreneurs harbor a misconception that their business is worth a lot of money, so they'll easily be able to cash out someday—and that's really all that matters.

Take my father for example. He had three Century 21 offices. Around 2005 he was offered seven figures for them.

"Dad," I remember saying to him, "you're not going to take that offer?"

"Why would I when I can keep drinking from the well?" he said.

Essentially he had what I call a "lifestyle business"—he was living off of it, not leveraging it to grow, create, value, and sell.

Fast-forward to 2008 when the financial crisis hit. All of a sudden, many of Dad's agents were leaving. These dire circumstances forced him to shut down one office and then another. Now he has a small office with just a few people working in it. The value is gone.

The same was true for a good friend of mine who wasn't in the medical business. He owned a few hardware stores that grew to encompass multiple locations. Like my dad, he had the opportunity to sell for seven figures. Also like my dad, he didn't. Fast-forward to the present day, and larger names such as Home Depot and other big-box stores have cut into his market share. It's become so bad that now, in his midfifties, he's trying to figure out how to liquidate his assets.

Another physician friend of mine fell into the same trap. He ran a practice for many years and became a huge name in the industry. Like the others, he had an opportunity to sell but refused. Today, his once successful practice is a downtrodden, dilapidated building that has weeds growing out of the cracks in the parking lot.

As you can see, many small business owners—physicians or not—make the same mistake; they fail to strike while the iron is hot, instead hoping to keep "drinking from the well." Most of the time, this strategy backfires, and they end up with nothing.

That's why strategically planning in advance to build your business, build your assets, and then sell when the timing is ideal is absolutely integral. Timing is key.

More often than I'd like to admit, small businesspeople I've known have made it to the cusp of retirement, having spent decades behind their business, but by then it's worth nothing. It's grown irrelevant or dated or has been left in the dust by the competition. That's because they never thought ahead to strategize a solid exit plan—and they didn't get rid of the business when they should have.

WHEN SUCCESSION PLANNING SHOULD HAPPEN

You've heard the saying "begin with the end in mind," and nothing could be wiser when it comes to succession and exit planning. However, most entrepreneurs and physicians fail to do this. Many doctors, like the ones I just mentioned, are in their late fifties and sixties before they even give exit planning a thought. I won't say it's too late to start planning at that point because it's never too late, but it's true that the later you start, the less desirable the results. For instance, you might still have a business that's saleable, but it might not be worth what it once was. That's the beauty of starting with the end in mind—it lets you enter the game knowing exactly when you should get ready to exit.

I know how tough it is. You have a practice. You're flying solo as a physician. At the same time, you're trying to drum in business from other revenue streams. When you're so bogged down in the day to day, when do you find time to think about the future? By being extremely intentional and mapping out your strategy from day one. Here are some questions to ask yourself to get started:

- Who will buy my practice?

- Who will buy my stock?

- Am I ready to sell?

- When *will* I be ready to exit?

Once you have the answers to the above questions, it's time to start planning strategically and in sync with your answers. For instance, the answer to the question "who will buy my practice" really yields only a few options.

First, you could be bought out by partners. If that's your goal, you should set out to attract this audience so that they're enticed to buy your stock or be a part of your practice. (We'll talk about how to do that in just a moment.) If that's your desire, you must add value on a regular basis by growing your business so that those who decide to become partners feel confident in their decision. Simply bringing on a partner and then growing complacent until you coast over the finish line isn't only unfair to your partners but can also result in a reduction of the share value of your remaining stock.

Your alternative to attracting partners is to gain the attention of either private equity or investors through an MSO, or management service organization. Nonphysicians can't necessarily own a medical practice if they don't practice medicine and aren't medical professionals. But they can own an MSO, which is a management company that manages your practice. The prospect of selling to investors is particularly appealing to people because they can make a lot more money from these sales. However, private equity or outside investors will only be interested in your practice if you have a well-run business with clean accounting and legal—an important point to keep in mind.

HOW TO ATTRACT PARTNERS

To make your practice appealing to partners, one of the strategies you could adopt is to target specifically those who complement what you do. For instance, if you're a dermatologist or a facial plastic surgeon, you could set your sights on bringing in a plastic surgeon. A set revenue stream and established patient base in itself is enough to entice partners—because they know they can feed immediately from your existing business.

For instance, if I'm a facial plastic surgeon and every fourth patient is asking for breast augmentations, I might focus on attracting a breast surgeon. The upside for this individual would be that they can immediately start pulling patients off my existing roster without having to put in the time or effort to curate their own patient list. This is a value add for them.

However, attracting partners is just the first step. Once you bait them in, you still have to keep them hooked. It's your responsibility to make the partnership attractive and sustainable by continually adding value, growth, and profitability to increase the worth of your stock over time. In essence, you're creating a deliberate win-win situation.

To achieve this, the first step is to ensure that you have a good business. As we've discussed, systems, policies, and culture are the formula to developing a robust business.

Second, you can leverage tools such as marketing and creating an online presence to increase your visibility and become a recognized name in the industry—a name people are proud to be a part of.

Third, you can invest in technology or equipment that speaks to your target's interests. For instance, if you have many operating rooms, this may appeal to potential partners who don't want to burn through their own dollars to set up an operating area. You want them thinking, "Hey, if I join John's practice, I don't have to worry about the operating rooms—they're already a part of the deal."

Baiting and keeping talent is a great starter step. But then you have to take it one step further to make that person a part of your exit plan—after all, that's what these efforts are all about.

Show them how the practice provides added benefits. Say, for instance, your partner has a dislike for management, which isn't uncommon among even the best surgeons and doctors. You can spark their interest by telling them that when they come to work with you, they'll never have to deal with the business aspect of the practice and will instead experience all the benefits of being an owner, including a well-designed retirement plan. For someone who doesn't have the stomach for the day-to-day hassles of running a business, this works beautifully. I've seen doctors attract other doctors who've previously suffered through bankruptcy—not because they were terrible doctors but because they simply didn't have the knack to run a business.

At some point, you'll also need to mentor and cultivate your successor, which is another lengthy discussion but one that shouldn't be overlooked. Don't leave this task for the last moment because it's not a job everyone is capable of doing well.

One word of caution throughout this entire process is that while you're out attracting the right people, don't forget to select the right ones too. This isn't a one-sided process where only one party should benefit. While you certainly want to ensure the prospect of joining you is appealing to the partner, you should also ensure that having them on board is equally as beneficial for you—and your exit strategy. Bringing someone on who is not part of your culture will ultimately lead to failure and wasted time. As someone who's made this mistake and paid for it dearly, I know all about this pitfall.

How to Select the Right People

Selecting the right candidate means choosing to work with those who complement your goals, your culture, and your vision. For instance, you don't want to bring on someone who has an ego or entitlement issues because this could end up hurting you more than helping the situation.

The first surgeon I attracted twenty years ago stayed with us for about a year and a half. Bringing him on and losing him cost me multiple six figures, not to mention my peace of mind. The surgeon was a great guy and a talented professional. But he was also a terrible businessman who had atrocious entitlement issues. He believed he was due much more than he was being given. We always caved to his whims, handing him practically whatever he demanded. He felt he should be paid more and that the staff should cater to him more than they did to me. He even insisted on having us pay for a separate phone line for him. My staff caught wind of his demands and was appalled by them. One of them came to me and said, "Dr. Williams, why does he have his own line? His phone never ever rings!"

When I'd coach him on simple best practices, he'd plain out refuse to consider them.

"Chris," I said to him once, "can you make sure you go to every ER at the change of a shift to introduce yourself to the patient?"

"I'm not going to sell myself like that," he'd scoffed. "I'm a surgeon. I've gone through all the training, and I know what to do."

In the end I realized he was a much greater liability than an asset. In my excitement with *attracting* the right talent, I forgot to ensure I was *selecting* the right person.

That's why an important part of the strategy is not only to entice the right people but also to be vigorous in your selection and vetting processes.

Retain the Right People

Once you've attracted and selected the right person, you need to make sure they stay on board. It does you no good to expend time, energy, and money if you're not able to keep them after you've gone through the effort of drawing them to you. Several key factors will help you with these retention efforts.

Maintain Clear Communication

Crystal clear communication is a must from the onset—that goes for any relationship. I have a partner who's been with me for twelve years. When he first joined our practice, I pulled him into my office to show him the books. "Look at this," I told him. "These are our profit margins."

He was completely taken by surprise. "I used to be in a bad medical marriage," he admitted to me. "I had a partner who was dishonest and never showed me the books. I've never had anyone willingly take me through them before."

No one likes being left in the dark. As evident from this partner's experience, relationships not built on clear communication, transparency, and honesty don't stand the test of time.

Be Fair

We know that often the problem with being extremely fair, or a "benevolent dictator," is that you get stuck with the short end of the stick. In your attempt to be fair, you might get assigned the most patients or end up working two Saturdays more than your counterparts. But as a leader, it's your responsibility to set the example and be a champ about it.

> → But as a leader, it's your responsibility to set the example and be a champ about it.

For instance, say my junior associate has a one-hour case and I'm looking at a four-hour case that brings in significantly more revenue. Many times, senior partners will move the junior guy around. "Hey, how about you stick your case in the afternoon so I can start my big case early?" they'll say.

That's unfair, and it's something you shouldn't do—even if in the process you end up being the one to come up short and stay behind later so you can finish up. Remember, think long-term benefits, not short-term wins.

Be Willing to Sacrifice

To get you must give. In some cases, you may very well sacrifice revenue from your own pockets to fill those of your junior partner's.

For example, I gave up soft tissue work, my birthmark clinic, my hair transplant practice, and injectables. I'm more than willing to forgo a fraction of my income to create value for the other person so they actually *want* to be there.

This is an area where some of my peers fall short. One of my colleagues brought on seven junior partners at one time—not one of them stayed long enough to make partner. My colleague's lack of willingness to relinquish his ego and a small segment of his income has been the major roadblock to that effort.

Ask yourself: Why would anyone want to buy stock in a company where practices are unfair?

I'll give you another example. My junior partner and I have an understanding that if a patient decides to have a procedure, they should have it performed by the person they've had the longest relationship with.

A few weeks ago, he called me, concerned. "Dr. Williams," he said, "Mrs. Sosebee did a fat-grafting procedure with you seven or eight years ago, and I've been doing injectables on her for the past few years. She was interested in other procedures. I told her she'd need to go back to you, but she told me, 'Why can't you just do it? I trust you.' How do you suggest I handle this?"

"Listen," I said to him. "Let's not split hairs. Go ahead and take care of her." Sure, I could have made some money off the procedure, and I inarguably had first priority over her. But times like that, you have to move aside, look at the bigger picture, and build value for those coming in if you want to exit successfully and gracefully. The big picture is this: I add more value to the business for the both of us if I don't try to steal a face-lift or procedure from this guy today.

Deliver Value

As a leader part of your job is to attract and retain people by creating value. This means you should show them the benefits of doing business with you versus branching out on their own. But it also means you should show them the tangible value of what your business is worth—you can do this by focusing on growing not only your practice but also your profitability. Again, systems, policies, and culture are the way to add this value and drive the desired profitability and growth.

De-Emphasize Your Role as a Technician

This tip is particularly difficult for people who are overachievers, which most physicians are. You've grown a practice with your own efforts, but the key to making the practice successful is to de-emphasize your own success. In other words, take you out of the equation. If there's one big name responsible for your business's entire success, once that name is gone, the business holds no value. There's no way you can exit it successfully and profitably—because neither the business nor its operations hold value; a single person/name does. To de-emphasize your role, you must build up people you're bringing on and make them successful. Help junior partners achieve success. Give them your trade secrets. Help them attain the same levels of accomplishment you have. Psychologically this is difficult to do, but it's nonnegotiable.

Run It Like a Business

Make sure your practice doesn't just look and sound like a business—ensure it runs like one too. Perform effective strategic planning, marketing, and cost accounting. Ultimately, when you run it like a business, you'll deliver profitability to shareholders so they're getting a decent return on their investment.

Craft a Deal That's Fair for Both Sides

If you own 100 percent of the stock in your practice, you're entitled to fair market value for it. Your junior associate or potentially stock buyers, on the other hand, are entitled to pay a fair price for that stock and not overspend. The benefits have to be fair on both sides. One of the biggest mistakes senior partners make is that they don't establish numbers and fairness from the get-go—primarily due to lack of communication.

Suddenly a junior associate is around for eighteen months or two years before the partner says, "Hey, you know what? Let's talk about how buy-in works. By the way, it's half a million dollars."

The junior partner feels the numbers seem extravagant, so they hire an accountant and an attorney who both agree. "That's not a profitable business," they'll say. Or they might conclude, "That is a profitable business, but he's asking way too much."

Now you've got two years vested in some awesome junior partner who you weren't transparent with from the get-go. The next thing you know, they've left to join your competitors.

So what's considered fair? Typically, around five times your earnings.

At that number, the person who buys the stock would see a 20 percent return on their investment.

Say you're a senior partner and you have a junior partner. Your practice is doing $2.5 million gross, which means $550,000 in what's called EBITDA (earnings before interest, taxes, depreciation, and amortization).

Let's assume your junior partner buys 10 percent of your stock and say we're using five times your earnings, which puts your practice value at $2,750,000. At 10 percent, your junior partner will pay $275,000 for the stock. After three years together, let's assume the partnership grows. You go from having $550,000 to $700,000 in profits or earnings. Let's work the math backward. The new partner now owns 10 percent of the stock and receives a distribution of 10 percent of the profit or $70,000. That $70,000 distribution divided by the original value of $275,000 shows an annual rate of return of 25 percent.

Is that a good deal? Absolutely. Additionally, we structure many other benefits to the partnership, pushing the return rates up into the 45 plus percent range. With returns like that, how easy do you think it is to have prospective partners who want to join?

Running numbers and crafting a deal that's fair and makes sense for both sides—from the very start—is critical because in the end, solid planning can result in a win-win for everyone involved.

KEY TAKEAWAYS

→ Begin with the end in mind when it comes to succession planning.

→ Start planning your succession and exit early on in the game.

→ Set your practice up and run it like a business.

 ▷ It should be profitable.

 ▷ It should have high morale.

 ▷ If both of the above elements are present, that's a sign of great leadership.

→ Become formally educated in business.

CONCLUSION

As you're coming to the final pages of this book, I hope you've gained the insight, confidence, and knowledge you'd hoped to in pursuing a practice of your own. We've covered a lot of ground. You've learned about my own experiences and background with entrepreneurship. I've taken you through my personal experiences in med school and the unrealistic lifestyle expectations people hold physicians to.

We've talked about resetting the mind-set to think like a businessperson versus a technician. We've discussed the significance of leadership and how the fish truly does stink from the head.

We've addressed how systems and policies are the meat of your business and can transform it from a mere job to a turnkey operation that relies less on you.

Strategic planning, as we touched on, is a key part of your entire business philosophy; it's what gets you successfully from point A to point B so you don't fumble or get swept aside by the competition.

We've talked about augmenting your income through multiple profit centers once you master the art of running a single practice.

Finally, we touched on the importance of striking a healthy work–life balance and how to avoid burnout, which is probably the most important piece of all—or the pièce de résistance, at least. After all, if you can't enjoy what you do because you're too exhausted, it's only a matter of time before you'll be tempted to walk away from your career altogether. As you can see from the stories I've shared, that's not at all uncommon.

> → After all, if you can't enjoy what you do because you're too exhausted, it's only a matter of time before you'll be tempted to walk away from your career altogether.

I wish I could tell you all I've shared with you is absolutely all you'll ever need to succeed in your practice. Although I've done a lot of research and reading for my own edification and to share knowledge with you in this book, I can't say that this book alone is the be-all and end-all of it. Certainly what we've talked through are strong starting points you should consider when you launch your own practice. The advice I've shared should help you avoid common pitfalls and see you through many of the hurdles physician entrepreneurs face. But knowledge, as I've learned, isn't finite—and it's not meant to be. It's something to continuously pursue and continuously imbibe so that you can remain competent and ahead of the curve. It's not a thirst to be quenched with a single sip. So continue to drink from the fountain of knowledge, continue to get mentors, and continue to grow your mind-set and your skill set. Don't stop with the last page of this book. Let this be only the first of many more to feed and nurture your mind.

In the end, whichever part of your quest you're on—whether you're just starting out, well into your career, or nearing retirement—I wish you well. Remember, no matter how new or far out you are in your career, it's never too late to start on the path toward improvements. Having tried today is better than never having tried at all. You can quote me on that!

APPENDIX

THE PRACTICE
(INDIVIDUAL)

(S)trengths	
	1.
	2.
	3.
	4.
	5.
(W)eakness - To be eliminated	
	1.
	2.
	3.
	4.
	5.
(O)pportunities - To focus on and capture	
	1.
	2.
	3.
	4.
	5.
(T)hreats - To be aware of	
	1.
	2.
	3.
	4.
	5.

FORM 2A - Practice

THE PRACTICE
GROUP

(S)trengths	
	1.
	2.
	3.
	4.
	5.
(W)eakness - To be eliminated	
	1.
	2.
	3.
	4.
	5.
(O)pportunities - To focus on and capture	
	1.
	2.
	3.
	4.
	5.
(T)hreats - To be aware of	
	1.
	2.
	3.
	4.
	5.

FORM 3A - Practice

WILLIAMS CENTER PLASTIC SURGERY SPECIALISTS
Analysis of a Healthy Goal

3

	Write your current goal	Is this goal measurable?	Does this goal have a deadline?	Is the goal achievable	Revised Goal (if necessary)
Goal #1					
Goal #2					
Goal #3					
Goal #4					
Goal #5					

Form 5A - Practice

CREATE A HEALTHY POOL OF	GOALS FROM KEY ISSUES (GROUP)
ONE YEAR	**THREE YEARS**
Practice	
note: A healthy goal is stretched, but achievable.	It is also measurable and has a deadline.

Form 4A - Practice

The Strategy	Circle # 1			
	Obstacles		Strategies	
Goal		⇐ ① ⇒		**Result**
		⇐ ② ⇒		
		⇐ ③ ⇒		
		⇐ ④ ⇒		
		⇐ ⑤ ⇒		
		⇐ ⑥ ⇒		
		⇐ ⑦ ⇒		
		⇐ ⑧ ⇒		
		⇐ ⑨ ⇒		
		⇐ ⑩ ⇒		
Today's Date;_____				Target Date:_____

All those things that seem to oppose our goals are the raw materials for achieving them

FORM 6A - Practice

The Project Planner

Stragtegic Circle # 1 Goal: _____ Strategic Circle # 1 Result: _____

	Strategies	Who's Involved	Fiscal Impact	Deadline	Status Report Date:	Status Report Date:	Status Report Date:	Status Report Date:	Completi Date
1									
2									
3									
4									
5									
6									
7									
8									
9									
10									

Form 7A - Practice

9 781642 251067